RESUME GUIDE

RESUME GUIDE

HOW TO LOOK GOOD ON PAPER! RESUME WRITING GUIDE
FOR DIVERSE COLLEGE STUDENTS AND NEW ALUMNI

Marcia F Robinson MBA

February 11, 2016

ISBN: 0997131608
ISBN 13: 9780997131604
Library of Congress Control Number: 2016901659
Career Center Diversity Partners, West Norriton, PA

Dedication

This book is dedicated to my parents, Reginald and Cotelia, who inspired me to live a life of advocacy for learning and self-improvement — always with the goal of helping others and uplifting the broader community. Every day, they showed us how to be unselfish with knowledge and to embrace the transformative value of education.

ACKNOWLEDGEMENTS

No book is ever a solitary project, although it feels that way sometimes when you are mired into your twentieth draft after four years, and you still feel your project is far from perfect.

This book is dedicated to the thousands of students and new graduates with whom, and for whom I have worked and will continue to work. They have kept me focused, learning, researching and evolving. I want to also acknowledge and thank the career and human resources professionals with whom I have worked and collaborated over the years. They have taught me so much.

A special note of gratitude to Philip, Raz and Makeba for their ongoing inspiration, ideas, coaching, encouragement and support.

As with all major endeavors in life, we discover more about ourselves and our world as we travel the path to give life to our dreams. This project has done that for me. I wish you a career journey that is long and fulfilling, and encourage you to take time to revel in the simple processes of your life as it unfolds. I am glad this guide will be a part of your journey.

Marcia Robinson

"It's not about what you want to BE when you grow up;
It's about what you want to DO with your life"

Table of Contents

Foreword

This résumé guide was written with students and new alumni in mind. However, this guide will be useful for anyone writing their very first résumé or writing their first professional résumé, regardless of whether or not they are in college, graduating soon or a new college graduate.

I wrote this guide because I believe that even in the age of social media, a résumé is still one of the best ways to communicate who you are, what you have done, how you have excelled, what excites you and where you want to be. It remains a critical component in a successful job search. I am truly convinced that, more than anything else, the process of writing a résumé allows us to learn more about ourselves, our motivations and uncover who we are and what we want to share about ourselves.

If you have read any of my blogs over the last fifteen years, you know that I often speak about knowing and exploring one's personal V.I.S.A. Not the credit card, but one's own Values, Interests, Skills, and Abilities.

This guide and the writing process I share will help you do just that.

Learning more about who we are as individuals, in terms of our values, our interests, our skills and our abilities lays the foundation for the successful professional lives that we will ultimately lead.

Whether we are working for others or working for ourselves as entrepreneurs, it is our professional lives that will ultimately sustain us, our families, and our communities.

For all these reasons, I don't just see résumé writing as a chore but instead, I see it as a process that helps us uncover and find out who we are and then express this to others.

This guide supports a process that is exploratory, action oriented, inclusive, and empowering. The guide not only contains the basics of résumé writing but also creates the mind-set that allows you to take full ownership of all your future résumé revisions.

For the last fifteen years, I have said time and time again that we write our résumés every day through the choices we make. The earlier in our lives that we make the connection between our current activities, personal learning, and our future résumés, the more successful we will be.

Why I want diverse students and new alumni to use this book

The answer is simple. Diverse students and new alumni who are emerging professionals, do not often take advantage of career planning services during college.

There is no one reason for this. Primarily, I believe, students in general and new alumni of color are unaware of the valuable role of career planning in their lives. Having worked in college career centers for over a decade, I know that most of these centers are underfunded. In career centers all across America, well-meaning professional staff work very hard for their students, alumni and employer partners. However, some populations on college campuses and in the workforce, remain underserved in the areas of career and professional development. The result is a troubling higher unemployment rate among Blacks and Latinos than there should be. The US Department of Labor has data to demonstrate the issue.

"While the unemployment rate for African Americans fell substantially in January [2015] to 13.6 %, it remains significantly higher than the 8.5 % rate of November 2007, just prior to the recession." Source – US Department of Labor, 2015

Add to that, survey results from AfterCollege showing that 80% of the college seniors in the Class of 2014, did not have a job when they graduated. Many of those graduates were students of color, who on average, took longer to find employment. As the global economy becomes more competitive for human capital, a report produced by Oxford Economics lists the qualities employers need most in future employees. These qualities include relationship building, dealing with complexity and ambiguity, balancing opposing views, teaming and collaboration, co-creativity, cultural sensitivity and the ability to manage diverse employees. (*Source – Gallup News*).

This guide will help students and new alumni identify those skills, clarify their goals and write a résumé that demonstrates the qualities needed to succeed.

My goal for the last fifteen years has been to empower America's diverse students and new alumni with the knowledge to help them claim and own their professional futures. Their efforts and contribution will be critical as we work to reskill America and build a 21st century workforce.

What's included in this Résumé Guide

- General guidelines for professional résumé writing
- Step by step instructions for each section of your résumé
- Résumé FAQs identifying problems and offering solutions and strategies
- Action items to help work through every section
- Checklists for use and reuse
- Hundreds of keywords to grab the attention of recruiters
- Online resources to stay current on workplace and employment trends
- Tips on how to use the résumé writing process to prepare for interviews

———

INTRODUCTION

Congratulations if you have picked up this Résumé Guide: How to Look Good on Paper. It means that you are serious about putting your best foot forward by showing your education, skills, interests, and accomplishments.

Like you, millions of people looking for great internships, scholarships, and career opportunities after graduation pound the pavements, troll online job boards and peruse social media sites with their résumés in hand.

Unfortunately, many of those résumés will be less than perfect. Frankly, most of the résumés will be bad. Really bad.

Despite the tons of free résumé writing advice online, in career centers, and in libraries stocked with free job search resources, most students and new professionals will still do a last-minute rush job with their résumés. Many will dive in feet first and hope for the best.

After more than fifteen years in the career management and human resources profession, I have seen many of those last-minute résumé projects from job seekers as part of an application packet. Whether the application is for graduate school, an internship, a co-op experience, or for landing an entry-level job to begin a career after graduation, having a résumé is where it all starts.

You should know that most people delay the résumé-writing process. Not to worry. It's overwhelming to think about. In my work, I have always found the fear is more about the decisions that have to be made while writing the résumé rather than the document itself.

For example, if you are planning to attend graduate school, you are probably more anxious about getting accepted than you are about writing the résumé. You are probably more anxious about finding a good internship than you are about writing the résumé.

Rather than deal with the anxiety and frustrations around those decisions, you will probably just delay writing the résumé, which ultimately delays the applications. Before you know it, you are in a cycle of anxiety and worry. The bottom line is that there is no way around it. You have to just begin.

The key is to remember that the process is pretty straightforward and relatively simple. Writing your résumé will be much easier than most college classes you will ever have to take.

A little secret I share all the time is that the résumé is really just a summary of important things you have done and choices you have made.

If you have done nothing, then there is nothing to include in a résumé. Trust me on this. I have had to work with many students who are ready for commencement, but not ready for professional life.

If you learn nothing else from this book – learn this lesson early: If you are participating, doing things and learning things, then with a little bit of direction, planning, and help, you can have a great résumé that represents you well.

———

About the Author

Author Marcia F. Robinson, SPHR, SHRM-SCP, is an award-winning, senior certified HR professional with more than fifteen years of experience as an educator. During her career, she has taught, trained, and written about résumé writing, interviewing, the job search, employment, and workplace issues.

An MBA recipient with a concentration in human resources from California State Polytechnic University at Pomona, Robinson has focused on working with underrepresented groups including a diverse student population and new graduates in the college-to-career transition phase.

She currently lives in Pennsylvania and is the founder of Career Center Diversity Partners LLC. She manages TheHBCUCareerCenter.com job board where employers connect with a diverse community of students, new alumni and experienced professionals.

As a certified MBTI practitioner who has lived in four different countries throughout her life and career, she understands the value and importance of workplace diversity and inclusion.

Find her on Twitter @MarciaFRobinson if you want to talk higher education, business, careers, work, travel, gardening and politics.

———

THE POWER SCAN

As you prepare to write your résumé, it's important that you keep in mind who the reader will be and how the reader will view your résumé.

Remember that recruiters and hiring managers will give your résumé what I call the **Thirty-Second Power Scan!**

The recruiter's "Power Scan" is very similar to what career coaches call the "Thirty-Second Elevator Speech." This thirty-second speech is where you introduce yourself to someone in a quick, succinct way, including all the pertinent and relevant details.

The Thirty-Second Power Scan is what recruiters do when they read or glance through your résumé really quickly. Believe it or not, that's more than enough time for recruiters to know if your résumé or application belongs in one of three piles:

The "Keep" pile
The "Possible" pile
The "No Way" or the "Toss" pile

If the recruiter or hiring manager is busy, like they always are, they may even just eliminate the "Possible" pile completely, and send résumés straight to the "No Way" or "Toss" pile. This means your résumé could end up in the trash without a second look.

And it means there might not be a more detailed evaluation of your résumé, even if you are a great candidate. Recruiters will tell you that they miss good candidates all the time just because of how a résumé is written.

———

How to use this Résumé Guide

- Read through the entire résumé writing guide at least once from cover to cover.
- There are more than 60 Frequently Asked Questions (FAQs) about résumés in this guide. Once you have read through the entire guide, if you need to research a specific FAQ, just use the table of contents.
- There are sample résumés and letters to help you with the layout of your own résumé. Use any one résumé that has everything you like or use a combination of two or more.
- Save this guide so you can find it when you need it.
- Use the links provided in the guide to access additional information and online resources such as our blog at The HBCU Career Center where we share updated, details and trends in the résumé writing, job search and employment industry.
- Copy the checklists rather than use the original documents in this guide.
- This way, every time you update your résumé, you can reuse the checklists to double check your work.
- It is best to complete the "action items" as close to when you read the section as possible.

———

GETTING STARTED

Writing a résumé, is no different from writing any other document. There has to be some planning before you actually begin to put things on paper.

Before we get started with the writing process, let's look at the six basic questions everyone must ask themselves before they begin the process of developing a good résumé.

Why do you need a résumé?
This is the time to figure out and understand why you need the résumé now.

Some of the typical answers we hear from college students and new alumni for needing a résumé are listed below. Select the ones that apply to you.

There is space for you to come up with other reasons.

- ☐ I am looking for an internship or co-op experience.
- ☐ This is a writing assignment for a class.
- ☐ I am doing a résumé critique in the career center on campus.
- ☐ My college application requires me to submit a résumé.
- ☐ Scholarship applications require my résumé.
- ☐ I am looking for a summer job or part-time job.
- ☐ I am looking to start a career after commencement.
- ☐ I am applying for a new position at work.
- ☐ _____
- ☐ _____

What specifically are you hoping the résumé will accomplish for you?

Be very clear and specific with your answer. For example:

- ☐ I have a job announcement that I am using to apply for a job.
- ☐ I have a job description for a potential occupation.
- ☐ There is a specific graduate school program of interest to me.

This answer is not the objective statement you will write for your résumé. (And yes, I still believe that students and new alumni should use an objective statement on a résumé. You will see advice to the contrary, but I think it is the way to go for emerging professionals).

State the goal you want your résumé to achieve for you. When you are thinking of a goal for your résumé, remember that résumés do not get people jobs. It is an effective job search strategy and process that will get you job offers, not just a résumé. The résumé is just one step in an overall effective job search process.

Your goal must be specific.

Here are two examples of goals for your résumé and an opportunity to write your own goal statement:

- ☐ I want my résumé to help me get callbacks from employers.
- ☐ I want my résumé to show my eligibility for a specific scholarship.
- ☐ _____
- ☐ _____

What have you done?

Your résumé will log your past experiences, education, and skills. The experiences you share can be paid or unpaid.

For example, if you include your experience managing a college club on your résumé, it is most likely that you were not paid.

Volunteer work is also unpaid experience but very relevant.

I will be honest with you: if you haven't done much, it is hard to write a good résumé.

Hopefully it's becoming clear to you that *your résumé content is going to be a reflection of your involvement.* This is why I always recommend that students write a résumé in the freshman year of college or even in high school.

It is never too early to learn that we are actually writing our résumés every day through the choices we make.

Where have you succeeded so far?

A résumé will identify your accomplishments and outstanding achievements to date.

Once you learn the process, you will find yourself modifying your résumé as you grow your experiences. For example, after your sophomore year in college, you will find that if you have been participating and growing as a college student, you will no longer need to list high school experiences or accomplishments.

After your first year or two on the job after college, you will probably stop talking about your freshman and sophomore college experiences as well. That is bound to happen as you grow and excel.

The successes you talk about will evolve and so will your résumé.

What have you learned?

Prepare to write about your education and training. Résumés should identify all your relevant skills regardless of where you learned them.

After a few years out of college, you will notice that the college degree moves to the bottom of the résumé, replaced by work experience.

What's special or unique about you?

As you think about how to answer this question, imagine yourself as the reader of your résumé.

Your goal is for the reader of your résumé to "hear" your voice in your résumé. Yes, they will only be looking at the written word, but you will still be able to have your "voice" shine through. I will say more about making sure your voice is clear in your résumé in the FAQ about using professional résumé writers.

———

Three final thoughts before you jump into drafting your résumé

You don't need to be looking for a job to update your résumé!

Many people make the mistake of waiting until they are about to start a job search to write a résumé.

As a student or new graduate you will probably have classroom projects on résumé writing. If you do, keep updating the résumé document as you get new experiences or skills.

Don't worry about the length of the document as you add new things. Consider all the information you are adding as your "résumé inventory."

When it is time to use the résumé in an application, you will only use the relevant information based on your needs.

That means you could end up with a really long "résumé inventory" document as you organize this ongoing inventory of your past. However, you will develop the best one- (or two-) page document when you are ready to apply for internships, graduate school, jobs, or scholarships.

Know that recruiters can often spot résumés that were thrown together at the last minute.

Don't sabotage your own progress with a sloppy, last-minute résumé. These résumés are usually light on accomplishments and full of errors. Don't try to fool anyone by hastily throwing a résumé together. It will say more about your work ethic and attitude than you might think.

The last thing you want is for the recruiter to think that the poor quality of your résumé is an indicator of the work you will ultimately do for them. That's why it is important that you walk through this process without the stress of deadlines.

Résumés are a reflection of what you have already done and plan to do.
You are actually in the process of writing your résumé every single day with the activities you choose. If you choose to do nothing, your document remains a static list of "stuff" rather than a live document with current and relevant accomplishments.

Let's get started!

Seven Deadly Sins of Résumé Writing

As a broad overview and first step, I want you to think about the following list of general principles behind successful résumé writing. They are what I call the *Seven Deadly Sins of Résumé Writing*. These are just general and basic rules of résumé writing to keep in mind as we move through the process of writing your first draft.

Careless mistakes

We are all human, and we all make mistakes. Therefore, you should expect to make mistakes when you write your first résumé draft. It's just like any other writing project: you probably wouldn't want to turn in your first draft of something you wrote for a class.

Since all of us are prone to careless errors in the beginning, don't be afraid to ask for help with the writing, editing, or proofreading of your résumé. I got help editing and proofreading this résumé-writing guide. If you are worried about asking for help, this is the time to move beyond that fear.

Think about it this way: strangers (recruiters) are going to see your résumé and be critical of you as a candidate. Why not ask someone you know and trust to give you feedback on your résumé before you send it out?

Consult your campus career center, a friend, a colleague, family member, a professor, or even a former boss to help you critique your résumé so they can help you spot the careless errors. I'm not saying that your friend would know more about résumé writing than you would, but they can help just by offering a second pair of eyes.

Many online résumé writing services offer free résumé critiques and will catch some of the careless errors you miss. Research those services online. It would be a shame to be overlooked by a recruiter and have your résumé end up in the "toss" pile because of careless mistakes that you could have easily fixed. Don't worry about being judged. This kind of feedback is how all of us improve.

Irrelevance

Remember that résumés are not supposed to necessarily chronicle every single thing you have ever done. The goal instead is to package your most relevant, recent experiences, skills, knowledge, and accomplishments to suit the specific opportunity you are pursuing.

Very few résumés need to go beyond two pages and most student résumés definitely do not go beyond the one-page document. So if you find yourself going beyond two pages, recheck your document for relevance. Rule of thumb is that if you have a master's degree, it is perfectly appropriate to have a two- to three-page résumé, as long as all the information is relevant!

Lack of clarity

Your résumé should make a compelling argument about what you have done and what your goals are. Can the recruiter or hiring manager tell from your résumé what you really want? They should be able to do that.

Résumés should use statements that focus the document on your past accomplishments, present situation, and future goals. Don't waste your words on "résumé speak" or jargon that doesn't share any real information.

An example of "résumé speak" is repeating the term "Responsibilities include" several places in the résumé. Many people tend to write about prior jobs or professional experiences using this term. This is not necessary. Through this résumé guide you will learn how to use action verbs or key words to describe activities.

Imagine yourself as the reader of your résumé. Does it flow logically? Are the statements clear? If you were reading the résumé and didn't know the person, would you be impressed?

No marketing value

Don't forget that your résumé is like your business card. It represents you and your personal brand. Whether you are using email, fax, a niche job board or a company's Applicant Tracking System (ATS), your résumé will get in front of recruiters before you will.

You want to make sure that your résumé will represent you and your skills in a good way.

Professional presentation with an attractive and readable layout is very important on a résumé.

Fonts, formats, and styles should all serve to enhance and not detract from the marketability of your résumé. The sample résumés in this guide are a good place to start.

To illustrate this point about marketing, I always compare a resume to a movie preview you see before watching the main attraction in the movie theatre. The preview is a quick summary. It is visually appealing and is designed to make you want to get excited about an upcoming movie.

Your résumé plays a similar role. You want it to be succinct, visually appealing and make the recruiter want to meet you.

Writing style

Everyone has their own writing style, but there are some general guidelines to observe when you are writing a résumé. Try to avoid run-on or long sentences. Remove any personalization in the form of pronouns such as "I" or "my."

Some new graduates and even college students get professional résumé writers to write their résumés. This is an expensive option, but if you can afford it, be very selective when you are choosing a professional résumé writer.

Many professional résumé writers do an awesome job making résumés look terrific. No surprise there, since they write résumés for a living. However, be very wary of professional résumé writers who do not write in "your voice."

Make sure the résumé writer uses words that you would actually use. Make sure your résumé represents you, and not the résumé writer. Employers can tell the minute they speak with you on the telephone, read an e-mail from you, or speak with you at a recruiting event, whether or not your résumé really reflects you.

Lies or misrepresentations

Resume lies are becoming such an issue that almost 40% of Human Resources professionals surveyed by the Society for HR Managers, said they are spending more time checking references. Statistic Brain, a data warehouse that compiles data from many sources, says that 70% of college students say they would lie on their résumés to get a job. They also report that 53% of resumes and applications contain false information.

Do not lie or misrepresent the facts on your résumé. With today's social media and employee verification processes, lies on your résumé won't last. It's just too easy to fact check nowadays, and a good recruiter can spot discrepancies really quickly. The news is full of people who were fired for embellishing their résumés.

Represent yourself honestly. Lying raises your stress level and can destroy your reputation. If you lied your way into the job interview, it will show.

No outcomes

This one is a biggie! What's the purpose of the résumé if not to emphasize your accomplishments and outstanding work? Too many résumés document the past but *fail to actually speak of successful outcomes.* Believe it or not, that is what the reader is looking for: your prior successes. Recruiters know that the best way to predict future behavior is to look at past behavior. Therefore, recruiters are looking for positive past behavior that show outstanding outcomes.

As a student or new graduate you probably have more outcomes and accomplishments to speak about than you think you do.

That is the purpose of the résumé writing process in this résumé guide. It's to show you where your strengths lie, where you need to build your experiences, and what you have already achieved.

This process will help you clarify your own thoughts about your background. It will help build your confidence about your own knowledge as well as help you clarify what you need to learn.

———

5 MOST IMPORTANT PARTS OF A RÉSUMÉ

lthough you will see several variations on professional résumés, there are basically five essential sections that must be included on your résumé if you are a student or recent alumni.

These five most important sections are:

- Contact information: *Who are you? Where are you? How can we reach you?*
- Résumé objective statement: *What are your goals? What do you want?*
- Education and training: *What do you know? What have you learned?*
- Professional experience: *What have you done? Why did you do it?*
- Skills and competencies: *What have you mastered? How do you excel?*

We will address each section independently.

We will also cover many of the other possible sections that can substantially improve the résumé of a student or new alumni.

———

Contact Information: The Devil is in the Details

Having the correct contact information on your résumé is extremely important to moving forward in the candidate selection process.

You would be amazed at how many résumés end up in the trash because of offensive, unprofessional, or incorrect information in the contact section of a résumé.

If a recruiter is put off by an e-mail or website address on your résumé, it might not get a second look.

For example, a website address or email with words generally considered as political, religious, illegal, pornographic or violent, could most likely turn off a recruiter. Your résumé could just go straight to the "toss" pile.

It's similar to the reaction a recruiter will have when they research you on social media and find offensive information written by you or about you.

A recent annual social media survey from Jobvite (www.jobvite.com) demonstrated the percentage of recruiters reacting negatively to certain information in the social media accounts of jobseekers:

63% - Profanity
83% - Mention of illegal drug use
70% - Sexual posts
51% - References to guns

In the same survey, 66% of recruiters reacted negatively to spelling or grammar errors in social media.

This definitely applies to your resume as well. Therefore, it is important that the contact information is free of typos, errors, or omissions and at the same time be attractive enough to engage the recruiter or hiring manager in a twenty- to thirty-second Power Scan of your résumé.

Use the sample résumés to explore ways you could lay out relevant contact information so as to share all the relevant details without using a lot of space.

Your goal is to make the résumé attractive, easy to read, professional, and most importantly—correct.

*ACTION ITEM**
Regardless of which layout you use for the contact information on your résumé, use this checklist to proofread the section for content, relevance, and accuracy on your résumé.

Contact information item:

Telephone

- ☐ Are you using multiple phone numbers? Recruiters won't necessarily call and leave messages at every number. Pick one or two (home and mobile) at the absolute maximum. Do not use your current work numbers.
- ☐ Is your phone number current?
- ☐ Can you still be reached at the phone number indicated on your résumé? It won't leave a positive impression if the employer gets a message that your phone is no longer in service.
- ☐ Have you set up a professional voice mail?
- ☐ Does your voicemail have background music that is too loud?
- ☐ Is your voice mail in another language?
- ☐ Are there distracting sounds like dogs barking or traffic noises?
- ☐ Is it your voice, or is it the automated recording from the phone service provider?
- ☐ At the phone number you have listed, will someone answer who does not speak English?
- ☐ Will a child answer?
- ☐ Will the person answering the phone be able to take a message for you?

Email

- ☐ Does your e-mail address look professional?
- ☐ Are you using multiple e-mail addresses?
- ☐ Have you changed e-mail accounts recently?
- ☐ Are you regularly checking the e-mail account listed?
- ☐ Did you set up a professional e-mail account just for your job search?
- ☐ What's the security level on your computer? Did you lower the security level or check your spam or junk folder to make sure you won't miss e-mail responses from employers?

General

- ☐ Is your address above your name? Make sure your name is the first thing on your résumé and is in a slightly larger font than everything else.
- ☐ Are you using a font that is too small to be readable? Many résumé templates currently on the market use a default font that is sometimes too small.
- ☐ Is the top résumé margin less than a half inch? Contact information might get cut off if your résumé has to be faxed or scanned. I know faxing is old-school technology, but sometimes you still have to use it.
- ☐ Does your address take up too many lines when you have other important information to use? Limit the name and address to two lines.
- ☐ Do you have an adopted name or a nickname as well as your given name? Use both. For example, immigrants who do not have traditional English or American names, will sometimes adopt other names by which they like to be referred. Suggested layout would be to include your adopted name in parenthesis: e.g., Rosemary (Ginger) Thyme
- ☐ Is your name and contact information on all pages of your résumé?
- ☐ Did you aim for a consistent letterhead look of contact information for résumé, cover letter, thank-you letter, and reference sheet?
- ☐ Did you include a URL for an online portfolio in your résumé contact information? Do you have the URL for a LinkedIn account to add?
- ☐ Did you use both a permanent and temporary address if you are in college or relocating to a new region? One new trend in résumé writing is to eliminate your address completely, especially if you are willing to relocate for a job or do an internship in another city.
- ☐ Did you experiment with left-right alignment as well to improve styling? Contact information does not always have to be centered.

☐ Does the font in the contact information coordinate with the font used throughout the rest of your résumé?

☐ Have you used text boxes to save space when aligning text side by side in the contact information section?

☐ Are you limiting the use of graphics? Use small, appropriate graphic elements such as lines of varying weights for emphasis. For example, use a line to separate your contact information from the body of the résumé.

☐ Are you listing your social media profiles? Employers will check you out on social media whether or not you list a profile on your résumé. Whatever you list on the résumé, make sure you clean up your social media profiles accordingly.

———

Résumé Objective Statement: What do you want?

I magine you are a HR Director sifting through stacks of résumés from potential candidates for a position you needed to fill yesterday. You really don't have time to figure out what people are trying to say.

Résumés must grab and hold the recruiter's attention. This is why I recommend use of a résumé objective statement at the very top of a résumé. Some professional résumé writers do not believe in résumé objective statements.

Many professional writers believe that the objective statement is a waste of résumé space. I don't agree. I believe an objective of some kind is important to help set the tone for the résumé. However, I do agree that there are other résumé sections that could achieve the same goal as the résumé objective.

Some of the section headings you might see include:

- Professional Highlights
- Career Highlights
- Summary of Qualifications
- Profile

If you are a busy recruiter, you too would probably be wincing at overused résumé objectives (even well-written ones). These tell a busy recruiter nothing about you or your skills, specific goals, or potential value to the organization. This type of generic résumé objective typically won't get your résumé past the recruiter's twenty- to thirty-second Power Scan.

You should be using the résumé objective section of your résumé to demonstrate your immediate value and immediate goals. Be bold about where you want to be and what you have to offer. A well-written objective statement allows you to do that.

The following guidelines will help college students and new alumni audit and proofread the résumé objective statement for effectiveness.

Remember your goal: the résumé objective is most likely the first statement the recruiter will read. You want it to be a good introduction. A good objective can lead to more positive responses. After all, that is the primary purpose of the résumé: to get a positive response.

Be specific with résumé objective statements
If your goal is a job or internship, specifically mention positions, departments, and programs that interest you. State your preferences for a company branch location, regional office location, or a specific project you would like to work on. This is a good place to also mention your specific professional focus. Take a look at some of the objective statements in the sample résumés in this guide.

Demonstrate your immediate value proposition to the employer
The résumé objective is a great place to show what you might be able to do for the company in terms of improving the organization and their bottom line. For example, state your desire to work on enhancing a new company brand or helping to meet a specific fundraising goal. Being specific tells the reader you have done some research on the company and that you know what you want.

Avoid superfluous "nothing" statements
"Nothing statements" are usually well-written, grammatically correct statements without any real content. For example, saying "Seeking to make a good contribution in a part time job" is a nothing statement. It doesn't tell very much about you, what value you bring and needs more context.

Some statements can be longer and more complex, without really adding any context. This is clearly a case where more is not better. Why take the chance that the recruiter will have to read your résumé objective more than once to even understand it? You don't want readers to spend all twenty to thirty seconds of the Power Scan just trying to make sense of your résumé objective.

I have seen thousands of résumés with statements that are really generic and wordy. This practice will not make you a more impressive candidate.

Tweak résumé objective according to job requirements

No one résumé fits all applications and no one résumé objective fits all résumés. Make adjustments as needed to keep the statement meaningful depending on where you need to send your résumé. Make the connection between your résumé objective and the job description or the reason you are writing your résumé.

Avoid the one- or two-word résumé objective statements

"Management," "Internship," "Supervisor," "Part-Time," "Summer Job," and "Sales" are just some of the common one- or two-word statements that recruiters see as résumé objective statements. Use the objective to set the tone and flow for the rest of your résumé: the one- or two-word résumé objective will not do that. The recruiter's response to your one-word resume objective statement, is typically –So what!

Minimize use of personal pronouns such as "I," "me," "my" in the résumé objective statement

Many professional résumé writers advise job seekers to eliminate these personal pronouns completely from the résumé objective. However, I think it is acceptable to keep them if removing them would disrupt the flow of an otherwise effective résumé objective.

ACTION ITEM

Use this checklist to audit your résumé objective statement.

- ☐ Were you specific with your goal statements?
- ☐ Did you demonstrate immediate value to the employer?
- ☐ Did you avoid superfluous "nothing" statements?
- ☐ Did you tweak your résumé objective according to the application requirements?
- ☐ Are you using the one- or two-word résumé objective statement?
- ☐ Are you using personal pronouns such as "I," "me," and "my" in the objective?

———

EDUCATION, CERTIFICATION, LICENSES, AND TRAINING

The education section on the résumé for a student or new alumni immediately follows the résumé objective.

Keeping in mind that the top third (roughly 35 %) of your résumé document is the most important, you should list the most important information first. Just as with the objective statement, it is in this top section of your résumé that you really get to grab the recruiter's attention. If that doesn't happen, your résumé is likely to end up in the "Toss" pile.

Therefore, it is logical that your résumé objective statement will come just before your education. If you are in college or a recent graduate, this is the most important thing that the employer wants to know about you.

While you are a student and even when you are a new graduate, your education should not go to the bottom of the résumé or after your experience.

Some college students and new grads use résumé samples that were written for professionals with a lot of work experience.

These professionals often move their education information to the bottom of the résumé so that there is more focus on the work experience. This works for professionals with significant experience. The fact that you are completing or finished your college degree is the single most marketable thing a recruiter is considering. For this reason, the education information needs to be in the top one third of your résumé.

After you have landed your first job opportunity after graduation, you can be more flexible about where on your résumé you place your education and training.

*ACTION ITEM**

Use this checklist to audit the education information on your résumé.

☐ Can you name your degree or certificate?

Check with the registrar's office on campus or check your college catalog to find out the correct name of your degree program. You would be surprised how many students and new graduates don't really know the name of their academic program. Are you working on a bachelor of science in business administration, a bachelor of arts in business administration, or a bachelor's in business administration? Is it a BS, BA, or BBA? This is just one example. You should know this information and state it correctly on your résumé. It's the same situation with your high school diploma.

Some states and schools use unique names. For example, in the state of New York, there are two levels of high school diplomas. One is called a "Regents Diploma" and the other is a "Regents Diploma with Advanced Designation."

☐ Did you have a major or minor area of study?

What was your area of concentration within your degree? Did you complete a double major? Did you have a minor? Use correct program names and break out GPAs if necessary.

☐ What coursework is relevant?

When you are listing relevant coursework on a student or new graduate résumé, avoid repeating the subject names. Listing both English I and English II really means nothing to the reader and is a waste of space. Eliminate "I" and "II" and try "English, two years" instead. It saves space and gives a sense of advanced studies.

☐ Did you include nontrivial projects, lab work, and coursework that demonstrate your ability to work with teams or practically apply your knowledge?

☐ Did you participate in special training programs?

List all the educational experiences in reverse time order. If you are in graduate school, that should be listed first. Also indicate whether it is your first or second year.

☐ Did you complete a two-year degree and earn an associate's degree or a certificate?

☐ Have you included high school?

If you are in college, you can list your high school until you complete your college sophomore year. Unless you were a superstar in high school or you did something relevant to the application (e.g., ROTC training if you are heading for a military career or want to show leadership), leave it out.

☐ What about your certifications, honors, and awards?

Did you earn any certifications during your high school or college experience? Food Safety, CPR, or technical certifications like Cisco Certification are a great way to showcase a commitment to go above and beyond. Highlighting academic honors and awards you received will go a long way in setting you apart from other candidates as well.

☐ Did you include grade point average (GPA)? Is it a requirement that you put GPA on your résumé? No, it is not. Will it work against you if you omit it from your résumé? It very well could.

The fact is that recruiters want to know your college GPA. If your GPA is low, it is better to share that up front but have an explanation for why it is low rather than try to hide it. Without an explanation, the recruiter might second guess your qualifications or think that you have a poor work ethic.

You can share both an overall GPA and/or a major GPA if it tells a better story.

———

Professional Experience / Employment History

Once you have created a solid résumé objective statement and added your education and training, the rest of your résumé is all about providing supporting evidence to meet the stated objective. Once you have begun to lay that foundation with your objective statement and your education and training, you need to continue the story by sharing some of your past experiences.

The list below includes some of the types of assignments and experiences that can be included in the experience section of your résumé.

- Full-time, part-time jobs (paid or unpaid)
- Internships or externships (paid or unpaid)
- Co-op experiences
- Job shadow projects
- Volunteer work and community service
- Leadership roles in campus organizations

You will describe your duties and assignments for each experience. As you decide which items to include, keep in mind that you should understand the reasons why you did what you did. For example, if you work somewhere, you probably have assignments or duties. Of course your job is to do the work you are assigned—but you want to do more than that. You want to understand the reasoning and rationale behind the assignments and responsibilities you are given.

The statements on your résumé will have more impact when the reader believes you understand the work that you completed. For example, let's assume that you worked in a restaurant as a server. Was it a large chain family-style restaurant or was it a small take-out restaurant? In the large chain family-style restaurant, you probably were evaluated on how well you served several groups of people at the same time. In a take-out restaurant, you were probably going to be evaluated based on how quickly you served people. In one case, the company might be measuring your success based on the amount of dollars earned per table that you served; however, at the take-out window, your boss might measure the number of customers you serve and the amount of time it takes you to get an order ready.

Making it clear that you understand the "why" behind your duties will set your résumé apart from others. It is also how you will be able to distinguish yourself in the job interview.

General guidelines for this section are as follows:

- Begin every sentence with an action verb. These are otherwise known as "doing" words. They show action or demonstrate actual behaviors. Sample action verbs are words such as "served," "prepared," "created," and so on.

    We have included several lists of action words in this Skills and Competences section of this guide and three exercises about how to choose which words are best for your résumé. They are grouped by type of experience, and they will jog your memory about some of the things you may have done before.
- List your experiences in reverse chronological order. That means you start with the most recent or current experience first.
- Write in complete sentences, and don't list one-word tasks.
- Give the reader some context for your work. For example, if you worked in a retail environment, was it busy? Did it have high end merchandise? Was it a small store? Was it a large store with multiple locations? Context is really important as the reader evaluates your background.
- Include location information such as city and state. A web address may be used as well. The street address is not necessary.
- Do not include names of current or former supervisors or managers.
- Include the dates, and use the same format for all of them.
- Write about outstanding and observable outcomes.
- Use numbers and characters. Numbers (#) will break up the words and make the résumé easier to read. Characters such as percent sign (%) and dollar sign ($) will help to effectively demonstrate improvements, achievements, or outstanding outcomes.
- Use bulleted lists or short blocks of text.

Here are a few sample statements you might find in the experience section of a résumé for a new student or recent graduate. Please use the sample résumés in this guide to help you write about your experiences in meaningful ways.

- *Served up to 25 customers per shift in fast paced family-style restaurant.*
- *Created spreadsheets to account for $2,500 in event expenses.*
- *Developed marketing plan which increased membership by 15 percent over a semester.*

———

Skills and Competencies

The Skills and Competencies section of a résumé is where a reader will get a really good sense of who you are, how you have excelled and what you can bring. These words will demonstrate your strengths. Don't list skills and competencies where you do not excel.

For a new graduate with very little professional experience, this is where you get to tell a reader what you are all about.

We have included several Skills and Competencies worksheets with this guide. Use these lists to help you finalize the most relevant list of skills and competencies to include on your résumé.

Some tips for this section of your résumé:

- You can use this section to list skills you have, but have been able to utilize at work. For example, say you are a blogger, game designer, or web developer, but you have never had to use these skills on the job. This knowledge might not show up in the "Experience" section of a résumé, however, the "Skills and Competencies" section of your résumé would be a great place to add this information.
- One caveat about this section of your résumé: Do not claim technical or language proficiencies that you do not possess! It only takes a simple conversation for a recruiter to spot fake credentials, skills, competencies, and qualifications quickly.

    If you have limited experience in an area, it is much better to leave it off your résumé but mention your knowledge of a language or technical skill in the job interview. If you do use the information on your résumé, be truthful about your proficiencies.

- You can list your skills by writing a brief statement or sentence about each; or you can list words in an easy-to-read grid as you will see in some of the résumé samples in this guide.
- Use the Skills and Competencies lists in the back of this guide to help you develop this section of your résumé.

———

First Draft, Done!

I f you have gone through this guide you should have your first résumé draft completed by now. Once you have this information written down, take a look at the résumé samples that have been included with this guide for ideas to tweak the layout. If you are having major trouble getting started, just begin by following the template on page 170.

Hopefully you now understand that while you are going through this step-by-step process to write your résumé, you are also preparing for your job interview. This is why I urge students and new graduates to walk through this very process of personal exploration and writing.

It is not just about the résumé document. It's about your entire job search process and your personal career journey beyond that. All of it begins with your personal, honest self-evaluation of what you have done, what you love to do and where you could be awesome!

By the time you have completed your résumé, you have the words, the tools, the language and the knowledge of yourself to explain or clarify anything on your résumé during the job interview and, hopefully, in your career beyond that.

Once you have the first draft done, it's time to start sharing your updated résumé with people whose opinion you value and whose advice could help.

Although most of the people you share your résumé with are not professional résumé writers, you will still be able to get valuable feedback about the layout, flow, grammar, or readability. You will get a lot of information in the FAQ's about who can help you to proof read your résumé.

Don't be surprised if some of the people you ask to read your résumé also know about jobs, internships, or scholarship opportunities that interest you. Your résumé will always spark conversations about your career goals, your plans and the future.

———

FREQUENTLY ASKED QUESTIONS: RÉSUMÉ FAQS

I hope that working through this résumé guide has helped you understand that your résumé is more than just a piece of paper.

Your résumé is a tool that you can use to show your accomplishments, catalog your skills, and explain your goals. You will be asked to do all of these things in an interview, so writing the résumé is the first step in preparing for the interview.

Therefore, I want you to think beyond the words on the paper as part of your preparation for your job search and career success. If you understand the broader context of your résumé you will be more successful in using it.

I've been using résumé writing FAQ's for over fifteen years to help college students and new professionals understand the context and value of their résumés. As your career progresses, your values might shift or become clearer and your skill set grows. This is the rationale behind your résumé as an evolving, changing document that will represent your choices up until the present time.

These FAQs represent the most common questions I've been asked about résumés over the years. You will notice that most of the questions are related to how we actually use our résumés in the job search process.

———

Q1. Why do I even need a résumé?

There are many reasons why college students and new graduates need a résumé. As you can see from the list below, applying for a job is really only one reason to have a résumé.

You many need a résumé to:

- Apply for jobs
- Create profiles in Applicant Tracking Systems (ATS) on company websites
- Participate in on-campus interview programs in the career center
- Complete college and graduate school applications
- Complete scholarship applications
- Apply for special honor societies
- Apply for grants
- Gain membership to clubs and organizations
- Internships
- Secure volunteer opportunities
- Get part-time summer work
- Find a better job or get a promotion with a current employer
- Attend a job or career fair
- Conference application
- Create a social media profile (e.g., LinkedIn)
- Submit a proposal

One well-written résumé will work for most situations with just slight tweaking, depending on the requirements.

For example, if you are applying to graduate school, you can emphasize academic achievements. If you are looking for an internship or co-op, you can emphasize both your education and relevant experience. If you are looking for a part-time job, you can emphasize your prior work experience or your relevant skills.

———

Q2. HOW SHOULD I FOLLOW-UP AFTER SUBMITTING A RÉSUMÉ FOR A JOB?

I hear this question all the time. Most companies are not following up with all applicants directly anymore. The most you might get in response to your résumé is an automated message from an Applicant Tracking System thanking you for your application.

It is important to follow the instructions that the employer has laid out in the job posting. These instructions inform job seekers about the application process that the employer wants them to follow.

If you submitted an application at the job site or uploaded a résumé to a career website, the general protocol is that you have to wait to be contacted.

Many job search sites will send you automated responses to acknowledge receipt of your résumé and application. A few employers will publish a phone number or e-mail for follow-up. However, most employers will not.

If you submitted your résumé at a campus event or career fair, you should ask the recruiter for a business card. You can also check with the career center staff on your campus about how to follow up. They usually can give you tips depending on the specific employer or might even check your status for you.

If you are able to contact human resources at the company to get a status of your application, be polite and professional at all times.

Whatever you do, don't annoy the recruiter.

No matter what else you try, do not ask anyone else—your pastor, your professor, your congressperson (yes, I've been called by politicians) or your parent—to call the employer on your behalf. It will not make a good impression.

Don't stalk the recruiter on social media sites such as LinkedIn or Twitter. In fact, some recruiters will not connect with candidates actively seeking employment with their company. If you call, e-mail, or contact the employer once without a satisfactory response, continue your job search and explore other options.

As the old proverb says – Don't place all your eggs in one basket.

———

Q3. Can Graphics Improve My Résumé?

Proceed with caution when using any type of graphics on your résumé.

Just as inappropriate graphics on social media could impact your job search negatively, graphics on your résumé could do the same. Since recruiters will do only a twenty- to thirty-second Power Scan of your résumé, why take the chance that a graphic you like could be unacceptable to them?

Do you really want recruiters to spend any of those precious seconds on a graphic they may or may not like or understand?

If you are working in a creative industry, instead of adding a lot of graphics to your résumé, add a link to an online portfolio or a webpage.

If the graphic you are considering is a professional photograph, you might be eliminating yourself as a candidate as well.

Then again, things are changing in that regard.

For years we advised job seekers to keep their photos out of the job search, and now our photos are everywhere on social media.

If you have a LinkedIn profile, your photo is already online, so there is no need to add it to your résumé. I guarantee that if you're a serious candidate, the recruiter will be looking for you on social media.

Having said that, some simple graphics that can give your resume a more professional touch include: (Many sample resumes show how to use these effectively)

- Lines
- Bullets
- Text boxes
- Grids
- Asterisks

———

Q4. MY RÉSUMÉ IS LONGER THAN ONE PAGE. WHAT SHOULD I DO?

Résumés for students or recent graduates should really be limited to one or two pages.

Keep in mind that although you can have a résumé inventory of several pages, you are only going to include relevant information specific to that application process.

If you have had several internships or résumé-worthy experiences, it is acceptable to have a résumé that is longer than one page.

If you are in a STEM (Science, Technology, Engineering, and Mathematics) major or occupation, or if you are using a Curriculum Vitae which is just another type of résumé document (*FAQs #58 and #59*), expect to have more than one page.

To quickly shorten your résumé, try one of the following tricks that I used as a professional résumé writer for years:

- Limit your address and contact information to two lines only.
- Reduce margins to between 0.5 and 0.75.
- Reduce font size by one point or a half point.
- Use numbers like "75" instead of spelling out "seventy-five."
- Change résumé date formats from September 2005 to Sep 05.
- Double check that you are not repeating information.

In addition, think carefully about the reason you need the résumé and evaluate every item that you have included for relevance. I find that most résumés are too long because we might be including unnecessary information.

Remember too that your résumé is only one of the job search tools you have at your disposal. You will also be sharing information about your interests and specific skills in cover letters, through web pages, and through online profiles.

If, for example, you create a profile on a professional networking site like LinkedIn, you will be able to share much more information without worrying about space or length of the document.

Also, a cover letter will give you a good opportunity to expand on how your personal interests coincide with the company's values.

Some additional ways you get to share information beyond your résumé include:

- Social media sites like Twitter or Facebook.
- Job seeker profile on company career sites.
- Completed job application.
- Conversations at networking events like a career fair or information session.

———

Q5. Is creating a profile online at the company career site or on a job board website the same as creating my résumé?

Current technology allows us to create extensive profiles that share more information than a traditional résumé. This can be a good thing or a really bad thing. On one hand, these job-seeker profiles allow us to share more about ourselves in a less formal way.

However, this ability to share more information can actually get more people in trouble by sharing too much information or the wrong kind of information.

As I say to students and new alumni all the time, using technology doesn't mean we discard all the rules of professional behavior.

Therefore, if you are completing a job-seeker profile, stick to relevant professional information. So although these profiles are not quite the same as a résumé, they are an incredibly valuable part of the job search.

Here are a few things to watch out for as you complete your online profiles:

- In most cases the online profile has no limit to the length of sections so you won't feel restricted to a certain number of pages. There might be a limit with number of words, but it is usually more than enough for you to be sufficiently detailed. Please don't use this as an opportunity to ramble on with irrelevant information. Cut and paste from your résumé to save time.
- Most Applicant Tracking Systems (ATS, used by employers to allow candidates to apply for jobs online) won't alert you to spelling and grammar errors. It is always a good idea

to draft your responses in a word-processing tool like Microsoft Word or Google Docs first and then cut and paste into the job-seeker profile.

- You can actually be a bit more personal with your writing style for the online profiles. Imagine you are sitting across from the recruiter or HR Manager who is reading your profile online. It can be less formal than your résumé and more conversational.

———

Q6. Should the names of my references be included on my résumé?

No. The only name that should be on your résumé is yours.

Do *not* include names of references or former supervisors on your résumé unless the application instructions specifically ask you to do so. For example, some government agencies might specifically ask that you add a list of references including names and contact information with your application.

Think about asking the following people who are already part of your existing network if they would be willing to write a reference letter or be a telephone reference for you:

- Coaches
- Teachers from courses where you did well
- Faculty or staff advisors for groups where you are a member
- Career center staff if they have worked with you in multiple semesters
- Past employers, including campus job supervisors
- Supervisors or coordinators at a volunteer site
- Religious leaders like Pastors, Deacons and Ministers
- Family friends who are professionals
- Work study supervisor on campus
- Friends
- Leaders of your civic or community groups such as Girl Scouts
- Teachers of co-curricular activities such as band or debate society

Use caution when selecting which friends you will list as professional references. Make sure that the friends you select will leave the recruiter with a good impression of you.

Friends who graduated a year or so ahead of you could be a good option.

———

Q7. Should I put my photo on my résumé?

Unless you are in a profession where it is typical to include your photo, such as Sports or Entertainment, keep your photo off your résumé and cover letter.

Keep in mind, though, that if you post your résumé online or create a job-seeker profile on a networking website like LinkedIn or use social media sites like Twitter, Facebook, Instagram, or Google Hangouts, that your photo will be there already.

Remember that recruiters will check you out on social media: so change your photo(s) as needed if you are jumping into a serious job search.

Don't just change current photos; you might want to scroll back through recent photos over a few months or manage your privacy settings to limit what is visible to onlookers.

———

Q8. How do I post my résumé on a job board or a career website?

This is a pretty simple task, but requires patience and attention to detail.

Allow yourself some time because in addition to uploading your résumé, you might have to fill in answers to questions for an online application.

Most job boards allow you to begin the registration process, save your work, and then come back to complete the process if you can't do it all in one sitting.

Check out all the features available to you on the job board and use the ones that will give your résumé the best presence online.

I have seen the following features on job boards that you can use effectively in a job search:

- Search features to explore current vacancies by keywords, occupation, or location.
- Job alerts allows you to get notified via e-mail when jobs match criteria you have established (e.g., part-time or full-time internship). You can also get alerted if your résumé has key words that match key words in the job announcement.
- The ability to attach sample projects as well as your résumé.

Company career websites

Most large organizations today have their own job boards and online career centers on their websites. Companies use different names for their online career centers. Many companies link to their job boards from the top or bottom menu of their website home page. Some companies might require that you locate the Human Resources office online before you can access their job board.

As you do your research, here are just a few of the terms you can search to find company career sites. Here are some examples of organizations and the various terms they use for their career pages and job boards.

"*Careers*" – Xerox Corporation, Target Corporation

"*Career Opportunities*" – Vanguard

"*Careers*" and "*Diversity*" – Walgreens

"*Work for Us*" – Star Tribune Media Company

"*Human Resources*" – Western Michigan University

Another way to find the job boards for organizations you are researching, is to do an internet search with the company name and the word "careers" or "jobs." For example, search for "Bank of America Careers" and see what you will find.

You will notice, for example, that Bank of America has information on their career site that targets specific audiences such as, "Campus Recruiting" which speaks to working with college career centers to recruit candidates for jobs and internships. They also have information for "Returning Job Seekers" which could be for Veterans returning to civilian work or anyone who has been out of the workforce for a while.

———

Q9. What is the difference between putting my résumé on a regular job board versus using a *niche* job board?

Niche job boards or niche job sites are online job-search websites where employers can target candidates with specific interests. Niche job boards list jobs that are specific to certain industries, demographic groups, or geographical areas.

This way, for example, job seekers can increase the odds of connecting with employers in specific industries, with employers actively seeking to diversify their applicant pool or with applicants in a particular geographical area.

Job seekers can do anything on a niche job board that they can on other types of job boards. This includes searching jobs, uploading résumés, applying for jobs, and setting up job alerts.

Experts in the recruiting industry say that niche job boards help employers find a larger pool of targeted applicants.

Examples of *industry-specific* niche job boards:

www.opm.gov The Office of Personnel Management is where the federal government and agencies list their vacancies.

www.GIjobs.com A niche job board serving veterans and the military community.

Examples of *diversity-specific* niche job boards:

www.thehbcucareercenter.com A niche job board serving the students, alumni and staff of America's Historically Black Colleges and Universities.

www.nuljobsnetwork.org is the niche job board run by the National Urban League to support employment efforts in the African American community.

Examples of professional membership-specific niche job boards:

www.shrm.org The Society for Human Resource Management supports a job board for Human Resource professionals.

www.jobs.ieee.org is a niche job board for technology and engineering professionals.

These are just a few examples of niche job boards that serve a specific purpose and aim to meet the job search needs of a specific community.

———

Q10. CAN I USE THE SAME RÉSUMÉ FOR EVERYTHING?

I t is generally acceptable for everyone to have one good résumé that presents a compelling summary of one's skills, abilities, and achievements.

Once you have a good draft of a general résumé, it is easy to tweak for specific uses such as scholarship application, job application, or graduate school applications.

You can also find that you might have more than one general resume based on areas of interest. If I use myself as an example, I can have several versions of resumes that I can use depending on what I am seeking.

For example, I can have a different resume for each of the following:

Teaching: As a business faculty, I could develop a pretty extensive résumé with college teaching and professional training experience.

Entrepreneurship: As a Human Resources consultant, I can develop a résumé with focus on prior HR consulting assignments, company milestones, partnerships and projects.

Human Resources: In this resume, I could focus on my work in Labor Relations, Staffing, Recruiting, Training, Organization Development and Leadership.

Higher Education: For this resume, I could combine teaching, managing career centers and human resources in higher education.

As we grow professionally, and our occupational interests become clearer, it will be possible to have many versions of a basic resume. Most job boards will allow users to store multiple versions of their resumes.

———

Q11. WHAT SHOULD A GOOD RÉSUMÉ LOOK LIKE?

The sample résumés in this guide give you several options for what a good basic résumé looks like.

Résumé samples are a good guide to what your final product should look like. If you begin with the end in mind, you will find it easier to develop a good final product.

When you use a sample résumé, be creative and feel free to combine layouts. Just know that a good résumé not only has good content, but it also looks appealing and is easy to read.

In addition to the sample resumes in this guide, you can find many samples of resumes and letters, with good layouts on some of these websites by searching the terms below.

"About.com sample resumes"

"Susan Ireland sample resumes"

"Career Center at University of Illinois"

"Boston College sample resumes"

"Georgetown University sample resumes"

"thehbcucareercenter sample resumes"

Q12. WHAT ARE SOME OF THE POTENTIAL WEAK SPOTS I SHOULD LOOK FOR WHEN I AM WRITING MY RÉSUMÉ?

Potential weak spots on your résumé are those areas of the résumé that may grab a recruiter's attention but not necessarily for the right reason.

Examples of what I mean by weak spots:

Low grade point average

This is one I see all the time. You have everything else that the recruiter is looking for in a candidate, but your GPA is below a 2.5.

Break in education

For example, you started one college but did not finish, then you later enrolled at one or more different colleges.

Irrelevant or little experience

When, for example, the recruiter is looking for someone with retail banking experience, but your résumé shows experience in an insurance firm.

Gaps in employment

Recruiters get very curious when a resume shows a gap in time in employment history. This is a real hurdle for ex-offenders who may have been out of the workforce for a period of time. Gaps can be the result of a long term illness, caretaker duties or stay at home parent.

Whatever the reason for the potential weak spot on your resume, assume that the hiring manager will spot it.

My advice is to know where the potential weak spots are before you are blindsided with a recruiter's question. Prepare an answer!

Imagine, for example, you are on a telephone screening or SKYPE meeting with a recruiter who is looking at your résumé. Would you have a good explanation for why you have had three part-time jobs in a twelve-month period? Why you didn't participate in any campus activities? Why your GPA might be low?

If you have completed your résumé honestly, there may be areas that the recruiter has concerns about. Everyone has them, and you have to know how to respond when asked about them. If I'm applying for a job that requires three years of experience in retail customer service, and I've only had two years, that is a weak spot that I must be able to explain.

It could be that you have less than the requested three years' experience, but the two years that you do have were in a larger company or that you were promoted after a year. Therefore, you have to prepare answers to counter what the recruiter might see initially as a weakness.

It's your job to prepare an answer that will focus the recruiter on your strengths rather than on the weak areas, especially if you know you are a good fit for the job.

You must know the potential weak spots in your history and be ready to address those in the initial telephone screening or in the job interview.

Another situation that students and new alumni face all the time is when their GPA is lower than the employer's requirement.

When this happens, a job seeker should prepare an answer ahead of time that acknowledges the lower GPA, but also sells something else more positive to the recruiter.

Look at your résumé and ask yourself tough questions about the potential weak points.

College career center staff and interview coaches work through these issues with students and new alumni all the time in practice interviews.

―――――

Q13. What type of response rate should I expect when I send out my résumé?

A quick rule of thumb I learned from a career-planning supervisor years ago is to expect a 10 to 20 percent response rate for a résumé.

I find that is a good approach to take.

If you send out ten résumés, job seekers should expect one or two responses.

Of course this will vary based on the state of the economy, industry, profession and your qualifications.

In a bad economy, job seekers can expect lower response rates from employers so you will have to do more to reach out and connect with more opportunities.

The bottom line here is that the best way to know if your résumé is working for you is to start using it and see what kind of response you receive. If you aren't satisfied with the responses, then start asking why.

———

Q14. CAN I WRITE MY RÉSUMÉ MYSELF?

Of course! Everyone can write a good résumé.

I ran a professional résumé writing service for over a decade. I stopped writing résumés for people because I believe that writing a résumé is such good preparation for the job interview that everyone should at least work through the process of writing their own résumés.

With the right guidance, like the material in this résumé writing guide, you can develop a good résumé that will represent you well and get results.

———

Q15. IF I HAVE NOT WRITTEN A RÉSUMÉ BEFORE, WHERE WOULD I START?

You can start by saying, *I can do this*!

Since your résumé captures your academic and extracurricular achievements, you must be involved and present in the process. Do not believe the professional résumé writers who say they will do everything for you. That will not help you own your background or your experiences, and it won't help you learn how to sell yourself and your accomplishments.

With a positive can-do attitude and some help, you can have a good résumé that gets results. Learning about the process behind the résumé is invaluable, because you will write your résumé many times over throughout your career.

Read through these FAQs to get information on what works and what doesn't. Find a layout you like and begin to write your résumé.

———

Q16. Is a Cover Letter Really Necessary with My Résumé?

A cover letter is not always required. However, the general consensus is to send a cover letter, unless the job posting specifically states that a cover letter is *not* required.

If a cover letter is required or you choose to send one, here are some tips for a good cover letter:

- Your cover letter should be addressed to a specific person. It is never appropriate to use "To Whom It May Concern."

  If after research you cannot find a specific person to write to, you may send your cover letter using one of the following generic salutations:

  "Dear Hiring Manager"
  "Dear Internship Coordinator"
  "Dear Scholarship Coordinator"
  "Dear HR Manager"

- Mention the name of anyone who might have referred you to the company.
- Mention the company name somewhere in the cover letter.
- Ask for the interview in the cover letter.
- Refer to the specific position of interest or vacancy.
- Pay attention to spelling and punctuation. Use paragraphs.
- Use your own words. Don't use words you wouldn't use in conversation.
- Indicate what you can offer the company, not just what you want from the position.
- Make a connection between your skills and what the organization wants.

- Hand sign rather than type your signature if possible.
- If you are e-mailing your résumé, use the body of the e-mail to draft your cover letter. There is no need to send a separate attachment. This e-mail does not need to be too long.

Read more about cover letters in FAQ #18.

———

Q17. Is the résumé I use for jobs different from the résumé I might use for college admissions or grad school applications?

If you have a good résumé, it will work in both situations.

However, résumés for college admissions or graduate school should emphasize academic achievements and extracurricular or co-curricular activities.

Therefore, for your college application or grad school applications, be sure to include items like the following:

- Honors
- Awards
- Achievements
- Organizing activities
- Science fair awards
- Recognition for teamwork
- Conferences
- Alternative Spring Break experiences
- Publications and Essays
- Presentations
- Service Learning
- Community work
- Volunteer

- International exposure
- Research interests
- Study abroad
- Competition awards

———

Q18. What are best practices for writing a cover letter?

Recruiters can get a good sense of a job seeker from scanning a well-written résumé that illustrates a skill set, work timeline, education, and job experience.

They can learn more about a candidate through a simple cover letter that accompanies the résumé. The cover letter sets the tone and places the résumé in the context of the specific job and the company.

A cover letter does not have to be complicated. Since the purpose of the cover letter is to add your personal voice to your résumé, all you need is a simple cover letter to round out this portrait of you as an applicant.

These guidelines will help you pump up the marketing volume even in a simple cover letter.

Header on a simple cover letter should match header on a résumé.

This is easy to do with a simple cut-and-paste function. If you have the same header on your résumé and your cover letter, it gives the same professional finish of having your own personal letter-head stationery.

The header on your résumé already includes address, name, and contact information; so there is no reason to not use it on a cover letter.

A simple opening statement in the cover letter should mention how you found out about the position.

Recruiters like to know how you connected with their company. A statement in the opening sentence of the cover letter will achieve this. If you were referred by someone specific, this is a good place to share that information. Don't forget to also identify the position you are applying for.

Refer to your résumé, but highlight specifics in your cover letter.

The second paragraph is where you connect your skill set, education, and work experience to the company. To keep the cover letter simple, identify the top three most relevant things you want the recruiter to know about your qualifications for the job. These three bullet points will end up in the middle of your cover letter and will be easy to read.

A simple cover letter should still mention the company name at least two times.

Although you should keep the cover letter simple, you still want to strategically connect with the company. One way to do that in a cover letter is to mention the company name in the salutatory address information, in the opening paragraph, and in the closing paragraph.

Send your resume to someone specific.

Remember that your goal is to get more "personal" in the cover letter than in the résumé. You should address your cover letter to someone specific. A little company research will usually get you the name of a specific person to whom you should address your cover letter. If after doing your company research you do not have a hiring manager's name, find the name of the director of human resources. If all your research fails you, use "Dear Hiring Manager" as your salutation.

Your cover letter must have a strong conclusion.

No matter how simple you make your cover letter, the conclusion must be strong. It is perfectly legitimate to close your cover letter by stating your plan to follow up if you do not hear a response by a certain time. Include your e-mail and phone number in the closing section of your cover letter.

The following is a very simple cover letter layout you can use as a guide to accompany your résumé.

———

SIMPLE COVER LETTER

Your Name |Your Present Address |City, State, Zip Code | Contact information

Date

Hiring Persons Name, Title
Company
Street Address
City, State, Zip Code

Dear (Use a name):

First paragraph
State why you are writing this cover letter. Name the position, field, or general career area you are interested in. Indicate how you found out about the vacancy or organization. Refer the reader to your application or résumé.

Second paragraph
Clearly state what you have to offer. Why should the employer be interested in you. Mention one or two specific qualifications you think would be of greatest interest to the organization. Relate to the employers' needs for that specific job. Say why you are interested in that specific employer, location, or type of work. List key items as bullets in the middle of the letter.

Third paragraph
Mention that you plan to take the initiative in making the next contact with the employer. For example: "I will follow up within the week to confirm the receipt of my résumé and to discuss scheduling an interview." Restate your e-mail or telephone number. Thank them for their time.

Sincerely,
(Your signature)

Your Name
Title for yourself (e.g., College Senior, Accountant)

———

Q19. Aside from the five basic sections, what other potential sections could I include on my résumé?

There are many extra sections that you could add to your résumé to make it more impressive and customized. If you have spent your time in and out of the classroom in productive ways, you will have plenty of examples to use. As you gain more experience, you will begin to use many of the following categories to sort information:

- Professional Affiliations and Memberships
- Technology skills: web design, Internet research, spreadsheets, social media
- Internships
- Accomplishments
- Cooperative Education
- Training and Certifications
- Honors and Awards
- International or Global Experiences
- Leadership
- Scholarships
- Languages
- Interests
- Administrative Skills
- Summary of Qualifications
- Presentations and Conferences
- Publications
- Volunteer Work
- Community Service
- Military/ROTC

- Student Teaching
- Certificates
- Language Proficiencies
- Workshops
- Writing Examples
- Relevant Coursework
- Social Media
- Career Highlights
- Study Abroad
- Projects
- Teamwork: Band, Athletics, Greek

———

Q20. WHICH ERRORS ARE COMMON ON RÉSUMÉS FOR STUDENTS AND NEW GRADUATES?

There are many, many correct ways to write a good résumé.

Here are some of the errors that recruiters and HR managers consistently see on résumés from students and new graduates.

Spelling errors, typos, and poor grammar

Use "spell check." Just a word of caution: spell check won't find words that are spelled correctly but used incorrectly on your résumé. Good proofreading will do that.

Ask others to read your résumé to help catch these types of errors.

No accomplishments or quantification on the résumé

Here is a simple example of what I mean about not showing accomplishment or quantifying your outcomes. Look at the following two sentences:

"Served people in a restaurant"
"Served at least ten tables per shift in a fine dining restaurant"

The second sentence gives the reader more context about the kind of restaurant (fine dining), the kind of service provided (high level) and gives a sense of quantity of work (ten tables).

Missing dates

Add correct dates to your résumé using month and year format. Use the same format throughout the résumé.

Inaccurate or missing contact information

This is a major mistake made on résumés all the time. Have you sent your résumé out with an old phone number? Did you change addresses recently? Recruiters hate when they get a résumé they really like and then they can't connect with the candidate because of outdated contact information. Update résumés and contact information in online profiles frequently. One of the new trends in the workplace today is that many people are choosing to leave out their mailing addresses on their résumés. Instead, the focus is on a mobile number, e-mail, and LinkedIn account.

Poorly formatted résumés

One of the many errors that recruiters complain about is formatting errors that make the résumé hard to read. Some of these include using overly large fonts, using all UPPERCASE LETTERS, multiple font types in the same résumé, and different shapes and sizes of bullets. It just looks better to keep résumé format consistent.

Too long résumés

Recruiters don't really read your entire résumé in their first scan. Making sure the top 30 percent is impressive is a good way to capture their attention. Use bulleted lists and avoid long paragraphs to keep the résumé to no more than one or two pages of relevant content.

KEY TIP*

Read your résumé backward from the end to the beginning. This way you get to "read" word by word and don't get caught up in the content. You will definitely catch spelling errors this way.

Q21. Aside from this guide, where can I get help additional help writing my résumé?

There are tons of resources available to assist with résumé writing. This guide is one resource that can be used over and over again. The checklists are useful and can be copied and reused.

Other places to get additional résumé writing help:

- The career office at your college or university. For example, 98% of the career centers on the campuses of Historically Black Colleges and Universities serve students before and after graduation.
- Parents or other professionals who can also help to proofread résumés.
- Any human resource professional, recruiter or hiring manager.
- Employment agency staff help potential candidates improve their résumés.
- Job fair recruiters are also willing to help.

———

Q22. MY GPA IS NOT VERY GOOD. SHOULD I INCLUDE IT ON MY RÉSUMÉ?

This is one of the questions that students and new graduates ask me all the time about résumé writing. My first piece of advice is if you have a low GPA, know that you are not the only person who has struggled with GPA issues, and you won't be the last.

The fact is, your GPA is one of those little facts that employers and others will use to determine your skill level, work ethics, or your ability to learn new things.

So if your GPA is below a 2.5, you can pretty much expect the employer to assume that your skill level is low, that you have a poor work ethic, or you that are not able to learn new things. However, you know that isn't true; so your responsibility is to think about how to convince the employer that those assumptions are wrong.

There is a lot of debate about the differences between an "average" GPA from a really "hard" school versus a "great" GPA from an "easier" school. None of that debate matters for the purpose of my arguments here.

Ultimately, regardless of where you earned it, your GPA says a lot about you. Notice I said "*earn*," because whatever GPA you do have is the GPA you've earned.

A general guideline to follow is to include your GPA on your résumé if you have a 2.5 or higher. Some career staff would say include GPA only if it is a 3.0 or higher.

I actually believe it is good to include your GPA on your résumé no matter what it is, *unless* the employer specifies a minimum GPA requirement.

Why?

Put yourself in the shoes of the potential employer.

What if you were the hiring manager and saw an applicant with a "low" (under 3.0) GPA. What are some of the assumptions you might make about the applicant?

You could be thinking that the applicant is less committed, has a poor work ethic, or did not have a good grasp of the subject matter. All of which may be true.

However, in my years of experience working with job seekers, I know that this is definitely not the case in the overwhelming majority of situations.

Now, again, pretend that you are the hiring manager and are looking at a résumé. In addition to seeing a low GPA, what if you also see that the person:

- Changed majors while in college.
- Had a gap in education by dropping out and returning to school.
- Finished college early in three and a half years.
- Worked full time and during semester breaks.
- Had great professional experience through part-time jobs or internships.
- Completed a double major in college.
- Was very involved on campus.
- Completed a study-abroad experience.

Would any of these factors make a difference in how a recruiter might look at this candidate? The answer is-Yes!

It's not that recruiters only want to see high GPAs. They also want to see a good reason in a résumé for whatever GPA you earned.

I always share that the bottom line is that people need to own their GPA, regardless of what it is.

After all, you earned it, so own it. The main consideration here is that you graduated in the first place.

Is the job search going to be easier if the GPA is higher? In many cases it is.

Do you have fewer choices for jobs and internships if your GPA is below what the employer considers appropriate? Yes.

However, the key is knowing how to speak honestly to the potential employers about that GPA in context with all your other accomplishments. If you wait until the job interview to come up with the explanation for a low GPA it may be too late. Plan your response early.

If you are uncomfortable about how to answer questions about your GPA, contact the career center and schedule a practice interview. This will help give you the means to dispel employer's negative perceptions about you based on your GPA.

If you are not a graduating senior, you should be doing everything you can to improve your GPA or to create a scenario where a hiring manager will put your GPA in context along with everything else you have to offer.

———

Q23. Aside from a résumé, which other job search letters should I know how to write?

Although the résumé is the anchor to the job search, there are a few other letters that you should know how to write at this point. You will use these kinds of letters many times throughout your career.

The first is the cover letter which we discussed in FAQ #18. Each of the other four job search letters discussed here have specific uses for various phases of the job search. However, regardless of when each of these job search letters is used in the job search process, they do have some things in common.

- All job search letters must be addressed to someone specific.
- No job search letter should be addressed "To Whom It May Concern."
- All job search letters must be proofread for completeness and accuracy.
- All job search letters should be timely.

Current job search protocol says that any of these letters can be shared via e-mail.

Broadcast Letter

A broadcast letter is, as the name suggests, an announcement eg. announcing graduation from college and interest in pursuing a specific career path, an interest in changing careers or exploring opportunities within a company. The broadcast letter should include the reason for the letter. If the letter is being sent to a specific company, indicate specifically why that organization was selected.

Thank-You Letter

Thank-you letters are gratitude letters and are an essential part of a good job search strategy. The thank-you letter should be sent within forty-eight hours after a job interview or meeting. It expresses the job seeker's appreciation for the interview and the opportunity to get more firsthand information about the company and the job. For example, the thank-you letter could be the way a job seeker thanks the interviewer for their time or thank a networking contact for a new lead.

Acceptance Letter

Once a job offer is accepted, the selected applicant may choose to send an acceptance letter, to confirm details and express appreciation for the opportunity. This letter is a good time to ask about next steps.

Rejection of Offer Letter

Your job search has resulted in a job offer that you would like to decline. It's a good idea to send a rejection of offer letter to the employer briefly explaining the reason for your decision. You never know when you might have the opportunity to interact with the company again in another way, and it pays to build rather than burn bridges with a well-written rejection of offer letter.

———

Q24. Do I need a professional résumé writing service to write my résumé?

Everyone needs some help to write a great résumé. However, before you consider paying a professional résumé writer lots of money, use all the other valuable professional resources available. That includes this résumé-writing guide.

Here are some of the main reasons you will need help with your résumé and where you can get help. You might need help to:

- Proofread your work for spelling and grammatical errors or other typos.
- Assist you with layout and content.
- Find the best examples to demonstrate experience and skills.

Students have a lot of available help from their college counselors, career coaches, and from online resources. If you are a college student, your first stop should be the career office on campus. Ask a professor or a work colleague. The goal is just to get a second set of eyes looking at your document.

A good résumé will definitely get more positive responses than a bad résumé. So getting help proofreading your résumé is important.

As you go further into your career, however, there will be plenty of opportunities and hopefully funds, for you to work with professional résumé writing services or job search coaches.

The fact is that career advice and support is one of the services that we should routinely use in our lives, just like we do other professional services.

———

Q25. HOW DO I FIND A PROFESSIONAL RÉSUMÉ WRITER IF I CHOOSE TO USE ONE?

I know several new graduates who received professional résumé-writing services as a graduation gift. That's definitely one way to pay for it!

If you happen to be one of the lucky recipients of such a gift, here are some guidelines to help you find a professional résumé writer to work with you.

You should expect to pay for the service before even a word is written. Read testimonials, get referrals, and look for writer credibility and reputation.

Search in your local area with phrases like "Chicago résumé service," "Philadelphia résumé service," or "Detroit résumé service." Local résumé writers not only help with your résumé, but they are often connected with a local recruiters and hiring managers and might even know of local employment opportunities.

Work with professional résumé writers who have worked with students and new graduates before.

Use the best available resources in the career development center before you turn to a professional writer.

Look for affordability. In other words, you have to decide what you can afford to pay a writer to help with your résumé.

Be willing to negotiate. Sometimes in a tight economy, résumé writers are more than willing to be flexible with their rates.

Planning ahead will help you save. You can probably get better rates if your résumé isn't an immediate need. There are always writers willing to devote the time to work with you on your résumé, but you may have to pay more for a quick turnaround.

Professional résumé writers can assist you with cover letters, LinkedIn profiles, and other documents related to the job search. Find out about any free revisions or updates that the professional résumé writer will do as well.

———

Q26. WHAT SHOULD I WRITE IN THE E-MAIL SUBJECT LINE WHEN I E-MAIL MY RÉSUMÉ?

When e-mailing your résumé use a subject line that includes your name, the position name or number, the name of the company, and the date.

Sample: "Résumé Marcia Robinson MBA, SPHR—HR Manager at ABC Inc. 8-15"

Following a regular protocol will make it easy for either you or the recruiter to locate your most current documents.

———

Q27. What do I write in the body of my e-mail if I send my résumé as an attachment?

Millions of résumés go back and forth between employers and job seekers via e-mail daily.

There are three ways to handle sending your résumé via e-mail:

- You can use the e-mail as your cover letter and write the same things in the body of the e-mail as you would in a cover letter.
- You can write one or two sentences in the body of the e-mail and then attach your résumé and cover letter.
- You can restate your interest in the position and state the best way for the recruiter to connect with you.

Q28. Should I Use a Cover Page if I Fax a Résumé?

The simple answer is –Yes. Fax machines might be old school, but they are still definitely used. In addition to a cover letter that speaks to your attached résumé and other application materials, you should also use a generic fax cover page.

A fax cover page would include the following typical information found in a memo:

From: Your name

To: Recruiter's name

Date: 8-14-2015

Regarding: Application for the position of _____

―――――

Q29. SHOULD PERSONAL INTERESTS BE INCLUDED ON MY RÉSUMÉ?

Your interests can play an important role in your résumé. It is a good idea to include specific interests not noted anywhere else on your résumé, **but** only if it is an asset to prospective employers.

For example, let's say your goal is to work in the banking industry. An interest in the stock market and previous experience using accounting software as treasurer of campus group would be an asset. This may be a good opportunity to show that interest on your résumé even if you have never worked in a bank before.

Some personal interests and information should never be included in a résumé unless it is a legitimate part of your work history. Examples of these are as follows:

- Religious affiliation
- Political affiliation
- Marital status
- Date of birth
- Children information
- Ethnicity (Languages – Yes! Country of birth – No!)

———

Q30. SHOULD I SAY THAT I AM AN INTERNATIONAL STUDENT ON MY COLLEGE RÉSUMÉ?

International students with legal permission to work in the United States and/or those with dual citizenship should include a sentence to that effect on a résumé. It is a good idea to include start and end dates of your eligibility period.

———

Q31. CAN I USE THE SAME RÉSUMÉ FOR ALL JOB APPLICATIONS?

Yes and no.

With minor tweaking based on job requirements, your résumé can basically capture skills, knowledge, training, and education in a concise, marketable format that you will be able to use many times.

Your goal remains the same regardless of the position. You want to keep the résumé information relevant and to the point. However, some of the areas that might need to be tweaked according to a specific position include:

- The objective statement
- Relevant coursework
- Skills and competencies
- Professional work experience

Q32. How do I avoid stretching the truth on my résumé?

Lying on your résumé is unacceptable, but unfortunately recruiters will tell you that dishonesty about work history is becoming increasingly common. Challenger, Gray & Christmas, well-known employment experts, estimate that 10 to 30 percent of job seekers bend the truth or blatantly lie on their résumés.

Students and new graduates have asked me about the specific areas of concern listed below. Basically, my advice is to be honest with yourself. If you do that you will know when you are stretching the truth.

What are those areas most prone to exaggeration on the college or new graduate résumé?

Rounding up a GPA
It is acceptable to report a "3.14" as a "3.1" and a "2.87" as a "2.9." You also have the choice to use the GPA for your major subject only if it is a higher than your overall GPA.

Overstating technical proficiency
Many people list classes they have taken without regard to whether or not they have a good understanding of the material they studied. My recommendation is as follows: if you cannot have a conversation about the topic, remove it from your résumé. It's much more impressive to leave information off your résumé and mention it in an interview as something you have been exposed to, rather than put it on your résumé and stumble through a conversation.

Language Fluency

Increased demand for foreign language skills will entice some applicants to overstate their proficiency in languages on their résumés. State abilities clearly on a résumé with clarifying phrases such as "classes taken," "able to read and understand," and "conversational."

Dates

Some people misrepresent dates on their résumés to make it seem as though they have more experience that they actually do. For example, if the job application is asking for twelve months of customer service experience, it is tempting to change dates if you only have nine months of customer service experience. My recommendation here would be to be honest and apply with your nine months' experience. It is so easy nowadays to verify employment dates via the background-check process, so lying is not worth the stress involved.

Remember that employees are required to sign job applications confirming that all the information provided is factually correct. If an employer discovers that you lied or misrepresented yourself when completing the job application, that employer can exercise discipline, up to and including termination of employment.

———

Q33. With limited work experience, how can I make my résumé competitive?

Contrary to what most students and new graduates may think, no one really expects a college résumé or the résumé of a new graduate to show much professional experience beyond the following:

- Internships
- Cooperative education assignments
- Fellowships
- Campus organization involvement
- Community service
- Volunteer work
- Project coursework
- Scholarships
- Entrepreneurship
- Part time jobs

Although these are a few simple categories, you would be amazed at the variety of accomplishments that can be achieved in these areas. A résumé showing significant and successful participation in these activities will definitely get the attention of hiring managers.

Let me reiterate here that your résumé is a reflection of what you have done and who you are. It is a reflection of your brand. If you have done nothing, you will have nothing to share or promote. The key to a successful résumé, therefore, is to stay involved, learn, and grow.

———

Q34. WHAT ARE THE DIFFERENT TYPES OF RÉSUMÉS I SHOULD KNOW ABOUT?

Here are the fundamental four basic types of résumés. There are several résumé samples included with this guide that demonstrate different types of résumés commonly used by college students and new graduates.

Chronological résumés: Items such as education and work experience are listed in reverse time order.

Functional résumés: Experiences are clustered into major functional areas e.g. Customer Service, Project Management, Retail, etc.

Skills-based résumés: These résumés are focused on skills and accomplishments.

Combination résumés: These résumés use any combination of layouts that will showcase the information in the most marketable way.

———

Q35. AS A NEW GRADUATE, COULD I USE A FUNCTIONAL RÉSUMÉ FORMAT?

It used to be that the typical college student or new graduate would use only a chronological résumé. The functional résumé format was only used by senior professionals who were changing careers, reentering the job market or going back to school. This is because functional résumés focus on experiences in specific functional areas across occupations instead of on a specific historical timeline. For example, based on my background, I would have professional experience in three broad functional areas of Higher Education, Human Resources and Business Administration.

Within each of those areas, I would be able to identify specific activities.

However, today's college students and new graduates have such diverse experiences and backgrounds, it is perfectly legitimate to use a functional résumé.

With many people returning to college to advance their education and earn new degrees, college graduates are actually older on average.

Of course there is no one right way to write a résumé, and so whatever résumé format works for you is the one you should choose.

Explore functional résumé samples in this guide as well.

———

Q36. DO I REALLY NEED A RÉSUMÉ OBJECTIVE STATEMENT ON MY RÉSUMÉ?

I believe the résumé objective statement is necessary to set the tone for your résumé and demonstrate specific interest to recruiters.

However, you will come across contradictory advice from many professional résumé writers. If space is an issue on your résumé, and the objective statement is going to make the difference between a one-page and a two-page résumé, then by all means leave it off.

However, the résumé objective statement is a great way to highlight some very specific pieces of information such as:

- Departments or projects where you have an interest.
- Geographical or relocation preferences.
- Specific industries and professional areas of interest.
- Number of hours you are available to work.

A focused résumé objective helps recruiters glean information about you, your values, interests, skills and abilities as they do a Power Scan of your résumé.

Q37. I've written my résumé and had it critiqued, but I have had no interviews. Why?

G ood question!

Without seeing your specific résumé and the positions for which you applied, it is hard to say why you wouldn't be getting interviews.

However, consider the following:

- Are you sending out enough résumés? Are you applying often enough?

    A 10 to 20 percent response rate to résumé submission is a reasonable goal.

    The more résumés you submit; the more responses you will hopefully receive. Many job seekers think that one application per week constitutes a job search. It does not.

    It is a numbers game, and with online applications so common, it is easy to set a goal per day for applications. This is an important part of an effective job search strategy.

- Are you applying for positions without modifying résumé sections such as objective and experience based on the requirements?
- Is the résumé objective focused or is it too vague?
- Are you following the employer's instructions for applying?

    Some companies are very specific and eliminating even one step could have your résumé in the trash.

- Most importantly, are you working on a strategy to attach YOU to your résumé?

    You should know that no matter how good your résumé is; recruiters will respond to job applicants much more positively in person than they do by just looking at a résumé.

Look for opportunities to actually meet employers and recruiters face-to-face, on campus, at job fairs, during job search workshops, information sessions, classroom presentations, or off-campus networking events.

The more you attach yourself to your résumé, the more effective your résumé will be.

Don't hide behind your computer. Remember that your job search is not just about being online. You must make "on-land" connections too. That is why networking is such a key part of an effective job search strategy.

———

Q38. Are there recommended online resources for résumé writing help?

There are many services offering online résumé help for college students and new graduates.

Here are some tips for college students to find résumé writing and career help online:

- The website for your college or university career center should be the first stop for students who need online résumé help. Most career centers have online resource libraries and qualified career professionals who can help students via e-mail as well.

  Many centers now also have web-based career coaching services or software like Optimal Resume, that can easily be accessed via a specific school's portal.
- Look for online résumé help that is appropriate for college students and entry level employees or new graduates. Many services that offer online résumé help cater to more experienced professionals and charge fees only experienced professionals can pay.
- Look for local online résumé help. When you are searching the web, use the name of your city as well. For example, searching on "Phoenix résumé writing," "Philadelphia résumé writing," or "Miami résumé writing services" will result in a list of local resources.
- When you are looking for online resources, try not to only look for résumé writing assistance. Look for organizations, individuals, and associations that support students and college graduates in a holistic manner and look to help students with all aspects of career development assistance and job search support.
- Use government agencies like ONET or Career Link workforce development offices.
- Consider this list of my favorite twenty-five Twitter pages that I believe offer good information to help the diverse college student and new graduate with the transition from college to career.

Follow these Twitter pages, and you will have access to a ton of free career advice.

Why, in my opinion, are these twenty-five Twitter pages that diverse college students should follow?

- They include images of a diverse workforce.
- No issue seems off limits.
- They share *honest* advice emerging professionals need to hear.
- They stay current (a biggie for me).

Of course I want you to follow me on Twitter as well at @MarciaFRobinson. We are all about diverse students and new professionals starting good career habits early.

As usual, my lists are never in a particular order, because they are all equally valuable.

@UndercoverRec Undercover Recruiters, a recruitment and career blog.
@WetFeet_Career Career information about employers and market trends.
@GreatRésumés Résumé writer Jessica Hernandez shares tons of résumé tips.
@womenworking is an online career and lifestyle magazine.
@networkingman14 Art of Networking offers advice on personal branding.
@BCWNetwork Black Career Women Network: a professional network for women.
@NBMBAAhq National Black MBA Association.
@eddiefrancis Bridges the gap between your Greek life and professional life.
@Truaccess Tru Pettigrew is all about inspiring and empowering millennials.
@DailyMuse is all about seeking and finding that dream career.
@ChelseaKrost Radio show host who gives personal branding advice for millennials.
@OutforWorkOrg educates LGBT students and allies on workplace issues.
@HeyDrWilson Dr. Caleph Wilson speaks on STEM careers and resources.
@BOSS-eMag Education and entrepreneurial magazine for minority youth.
@AlisonDoyle Workplace, career, and job search guru
@DiversityInc Leading resource on workplace diversity management.
@FastCompany What's hot, what's current, and the future of business.
@LevoLeague gives career advice for designing a life you will love.
@TorinEllis is a recruiter who shares tips on job search strategies.
@NatUrbanLeague Committed to empowering African Americans.
@BlackEnterprise Promotes initiatives related to careers and business ownership.

@CareerSultan US Navy Vet who supports career and job search goals of other vets.
@Glassdoor Get Hired; Love Your Job. Salary, interview, industry information.
@NSBE Career advice from the National Society of Black Engineers
@BlackEOEJournal Helps corporate America develop a more diverse workforce.

———

Q40. WHAT IS A VIDEO RÉSUMÉ?

Let's face it, today's college students and new graduates are fully immersed in a video culture. They are indeed the YouTube, Vine, and Periscope generation.

Essentially, the video résumé capitalizes on the value of videos created to showcase skills and qualifications. The number of companies offering these professional video résumé services is growing.

The video résumé won't replace your traditional paper résumé, (we just aren't there yet) but it could enhance your professional presentation and brand. If you are using a video résumé, please make sure to follow the employer's guidelines closely for how to submit the video and what type of media is acceptable.

Here are some tips on preparing and using a video résumé:

- Dress professionally in business attire, as if you were going to a face-to-face interview.
- Keep your video résumé short–only about two to three minutes long. You can fit a lot of information into that amount of time. Think about your typical television commercial that only lasts thirty seconds.
- Look and speak directly into the camera, not at the desk or table below you.
- Make sure the lighting is good.
- Be mindful of the speed and pace of your words. You may need to do a few rehearsals and several takes before you have a video you like.
- Make sure there isn't any background noise and that the wall behind you isn't too busy or too stark.
- Practice what you're going to say ahead of time. Write a script and rehearse.

- Start by mentioning your name (first and last).
- Focus on your professional endeavors, not just your personal information.
- What you share about yourself should make you a distinct and unique candidate.
- Say why you would be a good employee and what you can really do for the company that hires you.
- Thank the viewer for considering you and share follow up information about how to connect with you.

———

Q41. WHAT ARE "KEYWORDS" OR "BUZZ WORDS" AND WHY DO I INCLUDE THEM IN MY RÉSUMÉ?

Keywords and "buzz words" are specific words or phrases that employers use to find candidates as they search through résumé databases or as they quickly scan a résumé.

We also use these keywords or buzz words when we are searching for jobs.

For example, if you are on a niche job board and trying to find internships, you might use the keyword "internship" as part of your search.

If you are studying marketing or you have graduated with a marketing degree, you could use keywords such as "branding," "advertising," or "creative" to help find relevant positions. If you are a biology major, you could use terms such as "STEM," "genetics research," or "pre-med" to get you the best responses according to your interests.

These keywords are usually industry or skill specific and used as search criteria the same way you would when doing any research on the Internet. The goal is to use keywords that are closely related to the opportunity you seek.

Ask career advisors at your school for a list of keywords that are relevant to your academic program.

The ONET resource at the US Department of Labor is also a great resource for researching specific occupations and the words used in the industry.

Use the Skills and Competencies work sheets in this guide to help you identify specific key-words or buzz words related to workplace functions.

———

Q42. How do I know what keywords, buzz words, or action words recruiters want to see on my résumé?

We have included several lists of keywords or action words in the Skills and Competencies checklists in this guide. You can also use buzz words that are common in a specific industry.

It bears repeating here that successful résumés require research. This research is not only going to be valuable for the résumé-writing part of your job search but will also be relevant for your interviews as well.

Why? The keywords you use in your résumé and in the job search are also the same words you will be using in an interview!

To put together an effective résumé with the most valuable keywords, will require you to read about and learn about the industries you like or want to know more about.

Remember that your résumé does not exist in a vacuum: it has to be specifically tailored the industry in which you are interested.

> **KEY TIP***
> Read the job announcement carefully and you will see keywords and buzz words to use in your application materials. Use a dictionary if you have to learn the meaning of words and terms.

Q43. SHOULD I BRING MY RÉSUMÉ TO A NETWORKING EVENT?

This is a good question. The answer is –It depends on the nature of the networking event.

If, for example, the event is a career or job fair, then of course you should bring a résumé. In fact, bring several copies for distribution to all the organizations you will meet.

However, if you are at a conference or at a "Meet-Up" event, there is no need to bring a résumé.

You can bring business cards or be available to connect with people on social media websites such as LinkedIn or Twitter even while you are at this type of event.

———

Q44. Is a LinkedIn profile the same as a résumé?

No. Your LinkedIn profile, like other online profiles, is different from your résumé in the following ways:

- Résumés are very formal documents where, for example, you would not use pronouns like "I" or "me." LinkedIn profiles are a bit friendlier and more conversational. Using pronouns is perfectly acceptable in your LinkedIn profile.
- Length of your information on LinkedIn is not an issue. Your LinkedIn profile allows you a lot of space to develop and show off your brand. You are not restricted to a one- or two-page document like a resume.
- Résumés are your words only, and the content is written by only you. Your LinkedIn profile could have endorsements from colleagues or references written on your behalf by current or former colleagues.
- Résumés have to be sent out to companies, but your LinkedIn profile is available, viewable, and searchable at all times.
- You do not include your photo on your résumé, but you won't be taken seriously if you don't add a photo to your LinkedIn profile.
- Updates on your LinkedIn profile are more about your input in discussions. Your profile is more about your current situation, goals, and future possibilities; your résumé is more about a summary of your past with some insight on where you want to go next.

Compared to your LinkedIn profile, your resume is very static.

———

Q45. How do I write a résumé in 140 characters like on Twitter?

Twitter is one of the most widely used micro blogging sites on the Internet.

When you set up your Twitter bio, you are actually sharing a little bit of information about yourself.

If you do use Twitter, you know that a tweet is 140 characters or less.

However, over time, people have become very creative in how they express or share more than 140 characters. Twitter users can share a lot of information about themselves through photos, header graphics, and direct messaging.

Trust the folks at Mashable.com to use the term "Twesume" to refer to Twitter resumes. Who knows what will be next as social media technology evolves.

It therefore becomes your challenge to capture the essential information you want to share about yourself with the world. Although your Twitter bio is by no means a résumé, you should think carefully about what you communicate to the world and potential recruiters.

You should be aware that if most recruiters or HR Managers are interested in you as a candidate, you can rest assured that they will be looking at your Twitter bio and your tweets.

Twitter résumé tips

1. What you post on the internet, can last for a long time.
2. Use your Twitter bio, tweets, hashtags and lists to tell recruiters what you are all about.
3. Connect to your LinkedIn profile or Facebook page in your Twitter bio. Caution on the Facebook page if there is personal stuff you don't want recruiters to see.
4. Pin a tweet to your page that speaks to what you are about. You can change that pin as often as you like.

———

Q46. WHAT IS THE FIRST THING YOU LOOK FOR IN A RÉSUMÉ FOR A COLLEGE STUDENT OR A NEW GRADUATE?

Speaking from a HR professional's perspective, I will answer in two ways:

1. If there is a specific recruitment for a specific job, the first thing I would look for is an immediate connection between the job requirements and the information you are presenting in the résumé.

2. If you are writing a résumé that is not specific to a job and exploring your options—as is the case for most college students and new graduates—then I am looking for certain general behaviors. These behaviors and competencies are at the core of what employers say they look for in new graduates.

Every year the National Association of Colleges and Employers (*www.naceweb.org*) surveys employers and publishes an annual list of the top skills employers say they want in new hires.

Here are the items that employers say were most important to them in the graduating class of 2014. Each item was rated on a scale of 1 to 5, where 5 is most important.

- Ability to work in a team structure—4.55
- Ability to make decisions and solve problems—4.50
- Ability to plan, organize, and prioritize work—4.48
- Ability to verbally communicate both in and out of the organization—4.48
- Ability to obtain and process information—4.37
- Ability to analyze quantitative data—4.25

- Technical knowledge related to the job—4.01
- Proficiency with computer software programs—3.94
- Create and/or edit written reports—3.62
- Ability to sell and influence others—3.54

KEY TIP*

Be prepared to demonstrate these behaviors that employers want in your résumé and in the job interview as well.

Q47. WHAT IS A "SCANNABLE" RÉSUMÉ?

To use a "scannable" résumé, is to use a document that can be "read" by a computer. The purpose of a "scannable" is the same as that of a traditional résumé: to get a call back from an employer.

Tips for creating a "scannable" résumé:

- Use a standard serif or sans serif typeface, such as Courier, Times, Helvetica, Arial, Optima, Palatino, etc.
- Don't use decorative fonts.
- Use a normal type size ranging from ten to twelve points.
- Use a maximum number of sixty-five characters per line.
- Avoid any graphics or shading.
- Keep formatting simple.
- Use uppercase for major headings.
- Avoid boldface, italics, and underlining.
- Do not use bullets or lines.
- Left justify all text.
- If your résumé is more than one page, put your name on top of every page.
- Print your résumé on a high-quality laser printer or inkjet.
- Use only white or pale-colored paper in standard letter size (8 1/2 x 11).

Q48. WHY DO EMPLOYERS LIKE THE CHRONOLOGICAL RÉSUMÉ?

Employers sometimes prefer the chronological résumé because the format typically shows increasing responsibilities over time.

Résumés in chronological order are easier to read with that 20- to 30-Second Power Scan. Readers can get a quick understanding of personal and professional growth and career progression.

Employers like the chronological order as well, because it is easy to spot credentials and also to spot gaps in education or employment.

A new graduate who is changing careers or returning to the workplace could have some challenges with this format if there are gaps in employment history. The functional résumé format would be a better option.

———

Q49: SHOULD SHORT-TERM JOBS BE ON MY PROFESSIONAL RÉSUMÉ?

Not every job you have ever had is relevant to your résumé.

If you are an adult college student who is changing careers, consider using a functional résumé.

A functional résumé is a document that combines similar job functions, regardless of where you got the experience. The relevant experience might not be in jobs that you had back to back.

Here are two ways to include short term jobs:

2002–2007 Retail Associate
Style Gap, Fashion Belts Inc., ABC Specialty

OR

Sales Associate
2002–2003 Style Gap
2005–2006 Fashion Belts Inc.
Summer 2006 ABC Specialty

Notice in the second example the gap between 2003 and 2005 is very noticeable. This applicant ended a job at Style Gap in 2003 and started a job at Fashion Belts in 2005.

This is acceptable if the work done during that period of time was not in retail and therefore not relevant.

Do not discard your jobs, regardless of how limited the experience was. As a former professor said to me, your background is what makes you who you are today. Therefore, all of it is important. Some of your background will be more relevant that others, depending on the position you are currently seeking.

A functional résumé is a good way to accumulate experiences that come from different places.

———

Q50. WHAT TYPE OF RÉSUMÉ IS BEST FOR A JOB FAIR?

Attending a job fair is one way to meet a lot of employers in one location. Since the rationale is to meet many potential employers offering many types of positions, it would be best to focus your résumé around the general skills and behaviors employers look for in college students and new graduates.

The résumé you distribute will offer a comprehensive view of your goals, experiences and skills.

―――――

Q51. Some recruiters don't want my résumé at the job fair. Why?

Many companies are now using Applicant Tracking Systems (ATS) that allow employees to submit their application information via online forms.

Decades ago, recruiters would collect hundreds of résumés at a job fair and then store them in large binders in the human resources office.

Next came the document-imaging systems where recruiters would collect résumés at job fairs, take them back to the office, and scan them into their databases.

Now, most large organizations have an ATS and will ask you to upload your résumés into their systems or complete their online applications.

This does not mean that the recruiter is not interested in you as a candidate.

You should definitely know that even if you apply online, recruiters are making notes on potential candidates they meet at job fairs.

———

Q52. WHAT SHOULD I EXPECT TO PAY FOR PROFESSIONAL RÉSUMÉ WRITING SERVICES?

It really depends on the type of services that you need. The cost of résumé writing packages will vary depending on the services being provided.

You can find résumé writing services that cost anywhere from $100 for a good basic resume up to hundreds of dollars for packages including résumés, letters, bios and LinkedIn profiles.

I have to say that as a professional resume writer for years, you won't actually always get what you pay for, so don't assume that the higher the price, the better the service.

The most expensive services won't always be the best service for you.

You have to really do your homework to make sure a professional résumé writer is working for you.

The upside is that even though some services can be relatively costly, you will get the opportunity to deduct many of your job search expenses on your annual income tax statements.

Keep your receipts and ask your tax preparer for help.

———

Q53. Is "fancy" résumé paper really necessary?

Not always. The content of your résumé is much more important than the paper it is written on.

Good résumé paper, like that produced by the Southworth company, does add a level of professionalism and makes a good first impression.

Take several copies of your resume printed on quality paper to an interview since you could end up having multiple interviews or doing one interview with a panel of interviewers.

———

Q54. I SEE THE PHRASE "ASCII TEXT RÉSUMÉ" WHEN I ATTEMPT TO UPLOAD MY RÉSUMÉ ONLINE. WHAT DOES THAT MEAN?

The term "ASCII" is an acronym for American Standard Code for Information Interchange.

In layman's terms, using an ASCII format will allow the recruiter to see your résumé just as you intended it to be seen.

ASCII uses a character set that can be interpreted by virtually every computer operating system and guarantees file compatibility.

One of the easiest ways to make sure that your résumé stays in the correct format is to save it in the PDF format.

———

Q55. I HAVE ONLY HAD SKILLED "BLUE-COLLAR" JOBS WHERE I GOT PAID HOURLY. DO I STILL NEED A RÉSUMÉ?

Yes. When I started a professional résumé writing service fifteen years ago, my goal was to bring professional résumé writing services to groups of people who had been overlooked by the traditional career industry.

There was little or no focus on workers in hourly skilled jobs, immigrant workers, vocational or trade school graduates, students (including high school) and reentry workers. I worked for years with those populations and definitely developed resumes for all levels and types of professionals.

Today, everyone is talking about reaching the underserved and that includes our blue-collar trades professionals.

- You should have a résumé if you are looking for full-time or part-time work in your existing field or a new field.
- You should have a résumé done even if you are changing jobs within the same company.
- A résumé is also necessary if you want to start your own business and seeking funding and other financial support.

Today's workplace is competitive, and therefore a résumé is an absolute necessity.

———

Q56. What if I never finish college? Will I still need a résumé?

Definitely, yes!

Too many qualified employees are overlooked early in the job search process because of poorly written résumés. You owe it to yourself to put your best foot forward. Regardless of whether or not you finished college you need to look good on paper.

Although you might not have a college degree, the employer will still need to see your skills listed on a résumé. They will also need to know about your past work experience; and the way you capture all that data in one place is by using a résumé.

Having a good résumé is a critical component in successful job search strategy especially if you are an hourly or skilled job seeker in a competitive marketplace.

Even if you did not finish college, it is important that employers know the extent of your training.

If you are currently enrolled and plan to finish your program, you can always use the phrase "Anticipated Graduation Date."

If you are not in a program currently, and you do not intend to finish your program in the near future, use both the start and end date.

Examples of how to write information if you have some college courses, but are not currently enrolled.

- Completed 24 Business Administration credits, Montgomery College.
- 30 Credits completed towards Associates of Science, Montgomery College.
- Montgomery College 9/14 to 12/15. Completed 48 credits.

———

Q57. What is a Summary of Qualifications?

The main purpose of your résumé is to market your skills, experience, interests and education. Your résumé should showcase your brand, so to speak.

One way to quickly engage hiring managers and maximize the success of your résumé in the first 20- to 30-Second Power Scan is to include a comprehensive "Summary of Qualifications" at the top of a résumé.

This Summary of Qualifications can have a few other names. Some of these other names you will see on résumés for this kind of summary are:

- Profile
- Career Profile
- Career Summary
- Professional Highlights
- Career Highlights

Regardless of what it is called, the purpose is the same—Get the reader's attention!

Résumé writers experiment with several variations on that same theme. Here are four key elements to consider.

Years of Experience
Summarize the years of experience and areas of expertise in your field. Remember that it is appropriate to add up all the experiences you have gained from more than one job and show a

grand total of time in a summary of qualifications. For example, let's say you work in customer service now and have been in your current job for two years. If you have another year of customer service experience from a prior job you had several years ago, it is legitimate to total up those years and state that you have three years of customer service experience for the summary.

Special or Recent Awards

Acknowledge any special or recent awards and professional recognition relevant to the position you are seeking. If you don't have acknowledgment from an organization, include an area of outstanding achievement from your last annual performance evaluation.

Add Certifications

Share industry-specific certifications or professional training that qualifies you for the specific position for which you are applying. For example, if you are applying for a supervisor's job and have recently completed a certificate in project management, this can be included in a summary as well.

Soft Skills

Identify soft skills that are difficult to quantify but that give you a clear advantage. These could include, for example, good public speaking, team building, and multitasking skills.

Examples:

Professional Profile: Writer, video journalist, editor, resourceful researcher and avid debater who has consistently worked since 2012 in a variety of multimedia and writing roles, seeking to land first professional journalism job in the greater New York area. Great ability to manage multiple timelines or projects. Areas of interest and expertise, especially at the intersectionality of Music, Culture and Politics; include Broadcast Production, Music or Video Journalism and Multimedia story-telling.

Summary of Qualifications: Excellent communicator, detail-oriented and creative professional with 5+ years' experience working on non-trivial projects in Marketing, Public Relations and Events Management. Demonstrated history of using excellent writing, research, collaborative and consulting skills to perform effectively in fast paced, dynamic environments while able to identify, analyze, and solve problems that garner successful results within deadlines and changing priorities. I have been consistently recognized as a reliable and dependable professional who worked steadily throughout college while completing competitive internships and assignments. I am currently seeking to advance professionally while exploring and supporting Diversity within the Arts, Entertainment, Non-Profit and/or Technology sectors.

———

Q58. Which is better to use—a Curriculum Vitae or a résumé?

A Curriculum Vita (Vitae is plural), also called a "Vita" (pronounced vee-tah) or "CV," (pronounced cee-vee) is a detailed summary of education, work experience, and professional activities.

The CV is typically accompanied by a detailed cover letter connecting an applicant's background to the position for which he or she is applying.

When trying to decide between using a CV versus a résumé?

- The CV is used primarily for applications in academia, science and research professions.
- Many applications for grants, fellowships, and scholarship specifically ask for a CV.
- If applying for jobs overseas, applicants may be asked for a CV since employers in other countries prefer to see more details than we put in the typical American application.
- The typical CV is much longer than a typical résumé. An application packet with CV, letter of interest, and letters of recommendation could be several pages.

Q59. What should I include when I am writing a Curriculum Vita (CV)?

If your application requires you to use a CV, here are some of the things you have to pay attention to, as you convert your résumé to a CV.

- The heading of a CV is identical to the heading on a résumé. It includes basic demographic details like name with educational credentials such as PhD, MSW and MD. It includes addresses (temporary and/or permanent), e-mail, telephone number, and any social media links such as a LinkedIn profile.
- An objective statement or a summary of qualifications may be used to establish the focus of the CV. The objective statement will address academic or research interest and connect with the program or job in which the job seeker is interested. Unlike resumes, CVs typically begin with educational accomplishments close to the beginning of the document.
- CVs list all education and training, including undergraduate, graduate, postgraduate, certifications, and continuing education coursework. It will include names of college or university and city location.
- List any outcomes from education including degree name, minors, completion dates, and areas of concentration. GPA if 3.0 or higher can also be included, as well as names of dissertation or thesis committee members.
- Include professional licensure, relevant certifications, educational or professional honors and awards.
- Scholarships, fellowships and special academic awards, including Dean's List, should be added. Include descriptions of the award as well as any dollars associated and dates of award.
- Details of grant funds secured should be included in the CV as well.

- Details of academic research and laboratory experience, including institution name, project, and even professors. Titles of research papers and any special techniques used should also be included along with details of theses or dissertations.
- Add clubs, memberships, professional associations, or societies.
- Include any presentations, publications or papers written or services performed during membership.
- Work experience and education information is shared in reverse chronological order on a CV. Included should be dates of employment, cities, and duties or responsibilities. Outline all accomplishments in some detail.
- Include strong technical and language skills.

Making the decision to use a CV or a résumé really depends on the purpose of the document. Regardless of whether you choose a CV or a résumé, the documents should be written to showcase skills and experience in the best light possible.

———

Q60. WHAT ARE EMPLOYERS LOOKING FOR IN THE RÉSUMÉ OF A STEM MAJOR?

Although there are differences in layout and style, all good college résumés include certain basic items. However, depending on your college major, there might be some specific sections of your résumé which could be of greater interest to certain hiring managers.

STEM is an acronym for Science, Technology, Engineering, and Mathematics and college students pursuing these majors, are very attractive to hiring managers right now. If you are a college student with a STEM major, here are a few specific tips for writing a résumé.

Projects
The projects included in the college résumé of a STEM student should be nontrivial projects. When writing about projects, be sure to include any specific lab equipment, processes, or outcomes from STEM-related projects. In addition to the lab skills, mention any team projects with fellow students or professors.

Research
Many college students in STEM majors partner with faculty on significant research while they are in college. This research involvement is great content for college résumés from STEM students. Include research experiences, on or off campus, as well as poster presentations or research methodologies.

Internships and Co-ops

Internships and co-operative experiences are important for all college students regardless of major. However, for STEM majors, internships are really significant. These experiences could be the competitive advantage that one college student has over another. Employers want to see that STEM majors are not just interested in their college coursework but also in the practical applications of their studies in real work environments.

Assistantships/Fellowships

College students with STEM majors who are considering graduate school should use summers to participate in academic fellowships at research universities. For example, the Duke University Institute for Genome Sciences and Policies (IGSP) is open to college undergraduates, even freshman and sophomores, with an interest in genome sciences. These are the kinds of opportunities that STEM students should be looking to include in their résumés.

The Department of Labor is projecting that college students with majors in STEM disciplines will continue to be in high demand for the next few decades. To stay competitive, students and new grads need to have strong résumés with evidence of research, projects, internships, co-ops, and academic fellowships.

———

Q61. CAN THE NAME ON MY RÉSUMÉ IMPACT MY JOB SEARCH SUCCESS?

At first this might seem like a strange question to some people. The fact is that some research has shown that résumés with names considered to be more "ethnic sounding" could have a lower response rate from employers.

In 2003, researchers from University of Chicago and the Massachusetts Institute of Technology completed a study called "Are Emily and Brendan More Employable than Lakisha and Jamal?"

They conducted an experiment by sending out résumés in response to 1300 job advertisements placed in the Boston Globe and the Chicago Tribune newspapers. Approximately 5000 résumés were received in response to jobs in sales, administrative support, clerical services and customer service jobs. The researchers measured the calls the fake applicants received in response to the résumés.

The résumés used were identical in content, except for the fictitious white-sounding names of Emily Walsh or Brendan Baker and African-American-sounding names of Lakisha Washington and Jamal Jones.

The researchers concluded based on responses from recruiters, that applicants whose résumés had white-sounding names were 50 percent more likely to get called for an initial interview than the applicants with African-American-sounding names.

The research revealed that while a White applicant could expect one response from an employer for every 10 résumés sent, an African American applicant would have to send 15 résumés to get one response.

The researchers found this to be consistent across all the occupations and industries covered in the experiment.

What does this mean for diverse college students and new alumni?

In an ideal world, all candidates would be evaluated based exclusively on their professional qualifications. However, we live and work in an imperfect world. I have seen hiring managers offer opportunities to candidates based on personal reasons such as attending the same alma mater, being in the same fraternity, sorority or church. It happens.

It means that during the job search, diverse candidates might be impacted by the conscious or unconscious biases of some recruiters and hiring managers. Think of this as another hurdle you will need to overcome. This means that diverse candidates will need to keep focus on goals, send out more résumés and stay more persistent in the job search.

The bottom line is that some people gravitate only to people who are like them. Others base their decisions on certain stereotypes about competencies. This isn't necessarily due to race or ethnicity, but could be a response based on the demographics of some occupations.

Keep focused on your desire to draft the best résumé you can and be as proactive as possible to get it in front of as many people as possible.

We should also make it our goal to recognize our own unconscious biases and how those could impact our own job search choices.

———

Q62. How can I show my diversity in my résumé?

This is one of the new questions I hear about resume writing from everyone, not just college students and recent graduates.

The American workforce is evolving. Changes in workforce demographics is causing more organizations to frame themselves as inclusive and welcoming. More organizations, including colleges and universities, are developing diversity initiatives and recognize this as a competitive advantage when doing business. Many diversity initiatives revolve around the organizations' access to and need for high quality talent to build a strong workforce.

Since the résumé is one of the main ways that employers engage with job applicants, this push to find diverse talent means that job applicants may be able to distinguish themselves on their résumés through their diversity.

In FAQ#61 I addressed some research that shows that some candidate résumés might be screened out because of the perceived ethnicity of applicant names on a résumé. In this FAQ, I am now addressing why you might want to purposefully demonstrate on your résumé the potential value to the employer as a diverse candidate. There is a difference.

In the former case, one's name is not a demonstration of value, beyond the reader's perception.

In this case, you are using your résumé to demonstrate how your experiences, involvement, skills, training and education could make you valuable to the employer. Here are some ways to do that:

- Detail any international or global experience such as study abroad.
- Show membership in any minority fraternity, sorority or professional minority organization such as the National Association of Black Accountants or the Society for Women Engineers.
- Speak to the value of diversity to you in a résumé Summary of Qualifications.
- In a cover letter, make the connection between the organization's diversity initiatives and your background.
- Show any education and training about diversity in the workplace.

There are no guarantees that demonstrating your diversity in your résumé will land you the job. However, if your research of the company reveals they are working towards a diverse and inclusive environment, then use your résumé to show your value.

———

Q63. WHAT ARE ACTION WORDS, AND HOW DO I USE THEM?

We addressed the use of action words, keywords and buzz words earlier when we discussed how to include professional experience on a résumé. We also talked about action words in responding to the FAQ about "keywords."

Action words are what we call "doing" words. They are verbs that actually speak to an action or activity. These words speak to behaviors; things we do. They actually also speak to skills and competencies that we have and demonstrate. Some action words could also be keywords, but not all action words are keywords.

These action verbs are used to begin résumé sentences when speaking about current or past work experiences.

Since these words are "doing" words, they are valuable because they speak to actually *demonstrating knowledge and experience.*

For someone going through the résumé writing process, these words can help trigger memories and recall assignments or tasks. These words are a great prompt for reminding someone of tasks they may have completed.

For this guide, I grouped the action words according to the type of work, skills and competencies you might be trying to describe on your résumé.

You will note that some words are repeated because they could describe activities in different types of jobs. For example, the word "coaching" can be found among the "helping skills" as well as in the list of "management skills" or in the list of "communication skills."

These action words are not just used to describe past or current activities.

Action words also help you determine the skills and competencies you must develop for the future if you are interested in a specific career or job.

Use the checklists to not only help identify action words that you can use to describe your accomplishments but also as a list of skills you want to develop.

The action word activities in this guide allow you to rate yourself on each of the skills and then document an excellent example of you using that skill.

Things to watch for as you use lists of action words:

- It is from these worksheets that you will be able to identify your personal strengths, weaknesses and areas for improvement.
- Add words that are not currently on the list but that work for you.
- Do not expect to use every word on the list.
- If you don't know the meaning of the word, look it up. This exercise is a powerful tool to build your vocabulary.
- You might find that you will have multiple work or experience examples for some of these words. For example, if you are exploring ways in which you have been creative, you could talk about a creative solution to a work problem or creative activities in a community theatre program.
- You might see a theme emerging to help you identify your strengths and weaknesses if you are using the same words over and over, or if you find your experiences are all falling into one group of words.
- These action words could be considered "skills" as well. If you don't have recent examples of you using certain skills, or if the examples you do have are trivial, you should find ways to get better examples that you can use in a competitive job or internship search.
- These action words will also become a part of your interview preparation. You will find yourself using these words in job interviews as well.
- Watch for these action words to show up in job announcements and job descriptions.

Action Words Activity #1
Your goal is to use action words to describe your current or past work experiences.

This exercise demonstrates one of the most powerful reasons why you should learn to write your own résumé. This exercise will help you identify personal skills and behaviors, use words that explain your brand and help you prepare for the job interview.

Step 1
Create a spreadsheet that looks like the Skills and Competence lists in this guide. There will be 3 columns – Skill/Action Word, Rating and Experience.

Step 2
To target your résumé for a specific job, read carefully a job announcement you like and identify 5 to 6 keywords or action words from the announcement.

Step 3
List those words in the "Skill/Action Word" column of your spreadsheet.

Step 4
Once you have identified the 5-6 words, use the "Rating" column to grade yourself on a scale of 1 to 10 where "1" means that you <u>do not</u> have strong skills in this area and "10" means that you have strong skills related to this action word.

Be careful here.

Sometimes people rate themselves really high, and then they are unable to identify specific examples supporting their ratings. For example, let us say that one of the action words you found in the job announcement is "collaborate."

Rate yourself on a scale of 1 to 10 as it relates to your role or work as a "collaborator." If you rate yourself an "8" that should mean you have great examples of how you have collaborated with others.

If you don't have great examples, within the last year or two, then a rating of "8" might not be accurate. By the way, the words you use here will show up in your resume and the examples you use will be shared in the job interview.

In other words, you might be thinking that you are good at "collaborating" and you want to put it on your resume. However, if you really don't have the examples to back that up in an interview, then your rating is too high.

Not to worry, it means that this is something you should work on. It means that if you are a good "collaborator", then you should be seeking experiences to demonstrate that behavior. That is how you will get experiences to speak about in the interview. If a career or profession you want requires "collaborative" skills, then your goal would be to actively seek ways to build those skills.

You should notice that by now, I have used several versions of the word "collaborate" in that example:

- collaborate
- collaborator
- collaborating
- collaborative
- collaborated
- collaboration

If this is a skill where you excel, it will show up many times in your language, in your résumé, in your letters, and in your interviews.

Recruiters will expect to see it show up in your behavior at work as well.

Step 5

Write about your best and most powerful examples of a time you exhibited that behavior in the checklist. For example, if you have rated yourself a "7" on the scale of 1 to 10, then you might have examples such as:

- **Collaborated** with campus organization to promote community service for chapter members.

- Worked with 5-person team to **collaborate** on creating new marketing materials for chapter membership drive.

Step 6
Repeat this exercise for each of the other 5-6 action words or skills and competencies you selected from the job announcement.

These examples become the core of the "experience" section of your résumé and the examples you will use in job interviews as well.

———

Action Words Activity #2
Revisit that list of behaviors employers say they want from new hires in the survey from the National Association of Colleges and Employers (*www.naceweb.org*).

Create another spreadsheet, listing the underlined skills and competencies in the list below. Rate yourself and add the examples. Your goal should be to keep making those examples more and more impressive.

- Ability to work in a <u>team</u> structure—4.55
- Ability to make decisions and <u>solve problems</u>—4.50
- Ability to <u>plan, organize</u>, and prioritize work—4.48
- Ability to verbally <u>communicate</u> both in and out of the organization—4.48
- Ability to obtain and <u>process information</u>—4.37
- Ability to <u>analyze quantitative data</u>—4.25
- <u>Technical knowledge</u> related to the job—4.01
- Proficiency with <u>computer software</u> programs—3.94
- Create and/or edit <u>written</u> reports—3.62
- Ability to <u>sell and influence</u> others—3.54

This process helps you identify the skills you need to develop so that you can speak comfortably in the interviews to share real examples to demonstrate your value.

> **KEY TIP***
> Remember my 3 C's of Successful Interviewing: Using excellent *Communication* skills to speak with *Confidence* about your *Competencies*.

Action Words Activity #3

In the previous action word activities, you looked at a job vacancy announcement and selected five or six keywords. You then looked at the list of skills and competencies employers seek in new hires.

For this activity you are trying to prepare a résumé for a future potential occupation, but you aren't actually looking at a job announcement or a job description.

Instead, you will be using the Department of Labor information for an occupation that you want to investigate.

Google the phrase—ONET (*www.onetonline.org*). I never remember the website, but always remember ONET.

You are going to use the Occupational Search feature and look up a specific occupation of Food Service Manager. The search response will be a summary report on the occupation which will include tons of information about the skills, tasks and abilities involved in this work.

Select three to four skills or abilities specific to that occupation.

Put those skills or abilities in the spreadsheet and repeat the steps of rating yourself and finding examples of actual past behaviors and activities.

What you have done is create a powerful career planning tool for yourself. If you are interested in being a Food Service Manager, now you know what skills and competencies are required. However, more importantly, you can now set some goals to improve or gain skills in those specific areas.

Once you have walked through this resume writing exercise, you will be preparing yourself for the interview by planning the best stories to tell.

This is how you end up with a consistent branding message across all of your job search communication materials, including résumé, social media profiles, and in the job interview.

Look for the "How to Interview Like a P.R.O." book in our required reading series to learn how to use this resume and occupational research to prepare for job interviews.

———

DO YOUR OWN 20- TO 30-SECOND POWER SCAN

N ow that you have completed a draft of your own résumé and read all the FAQs, the next step is to use this checklist to do your own "Power Scan" and evaluate your résumé the same way an HR professional would.

This exercise is even better if you do it with a partner in a résumé writing class or workshop.

If you are doing this by yourself:

- ☐ Don't look at your new résumé for about a week.
- ☐ Print it out.
- ☐ Set your timer for thirty seconds and begin to scan your résumé.
- ☐ What jumps out at you in thirty seconds? Errors? Edits?
- ☐ Make changes and fix errors.

If you are working with a friend or fellow student, exchange documents and critique.

Since your goal is to make sure you look really good on paper use the following checklist to critique your own resume.

This will take you more than 20-30 seconds!

20- to 30-second Power Scan Checklist

- ☐ Is the résumé easy to read?
- ☐ ASCII-type fonts? Eg. Times New Roman, Garamond, Calibri, Tahoma, Arial?
- ☐ Does it use font size 9.5 to 12 (except the name, which can be larger)?
- ☐ Are there balanced white spaces between sections?
- ☐ Are the margins even?
- ☐ Are bullets, boldface, underlining, and italics all used appropriately?
- ☐ Is there a clean overall presentation?
- ☐ Does it give you a good sense of the applicant in 20 to 30 seconds?
- ☐ Does it show enough about ability, attitude, or potential to do the job?
- ☐ Does the content support the résumé objective statement?
- ☐ Is it employer centered and not self-centered?
- ☐ Does it show knowledge of the field, career, or industry with buzz words?
- ☐ Does it have personal pronouns only in the objective statement?
- ☐ Are there 3 to 6 key achievements per job?
- ☐ Is there cumulative relevant experience?
- ☐ Are there distinctive accomplishments that support the résumé objective?
- ☐ Does it suggest behaviors employers want?
- ☐ Is the highest level of educational accomplishment listed first?
- ☐ Is there education/training listed in reverse chronological order?
- ☐ Are there degrees in progress or recently completed?
- ☐ Is the correct degree, name, and location of university indicated?
- ☐ Are dates of graduation or anticipated dates listed?
- ☐ Does it list degrees and relevant higher education coursework?
- ☐ Does it list continuing professional education or training courses?
- ☐ Does it include study abroad?
- ☐ Does it include major, minor, or areas of concentration?
- ☐ Are there impressive honors or relevant extracurricular activities listed?
- ☐ Does it include relevant coursework?
- ☐ Are there papers and projects listed? Are paper or project titles included?
- ☐ Are honors, awards, scholarships listed?
- ☐ Are there other achievements listed (e.g., % of educational costs self-financed)?
- ☐ If using chronological format, is the most recent experience first?
- ☐ Are there volunteer experiences?
- ☐ Are internships or cooperative education experiences included?
- ☐ Are dates included with a consistent format?

- ☐ Are there functions/responsibilities valuable to the reader?
- ☐ Are there transferable skills?
- ☐ Were there problems identified and solutions found?
- ☐ Were there outstanding outcomes?
- ☐ Were there plenty of action words throughout the document?
- ☐ Were there quantitative or qualitative indicators ($, #, %) of outcomes?
- ☐ Can you see any career progression?
- ☐ Were accomplishments described in industry language or buzz words?
- ☐ Are values aligned with organizational culture?
- ☐ Are interests clear and related to the future?
- ☐ Are skills a good fit with the opportunity to develop?
- ☐ Are abilities clearly demonstrated?
- ☐ Any current involvement and engagement with chosen industry community?
- ☐ Memberships?
- ☐ Leadership?
- ☐ Does it avoid racial, religious, or political biases except for BFOQs (bona fide occupational qualifications)?
- ☐ Does it omit age, sex, marital status, national origin, health, names of references, and/or immigration status? (Include these if requested.)
- ☐ Does the resume demonstrate your V.I.S.A. (Values, Interests, Skills and Abilities)?

———

SOME FINAL THOUGHTS!

"I am not getting any job offers, and so I need to change my résumé." These are words we hear all the time.

Don't blame the résumé if you are not getting job offers.

Those of us who work in career management or human resources often hear job seekers blame their résumé when things are not going well in a job search.

Of course, in some cases it is legitimate to blame the résumé if it is not well written and doesn't showcase skills and work experiences effectively. If you have drafted a résumé, received feedback on it, and are still not getting calls, then it's time to start doing some problem solving.

Once we begin walking through the steps you are taking in the job search, however, we often find that the résumé is not really the problem.

For example, if a job seeker is distributing résumés, getting calls, and not getting job interviews, there is probably an issue with that phone screening or your response to a recruiter via e-mail. If you are doing interviews, but not getting job offers, rewriting the résumé is likely not going to improve the outcome.

Job seekers should consider some of the following issues before blaming the résumé and launching into a major résumé rewrite.

What impression is the job seeker making during a telephone screening?

Rather than blaming the résumé, think through the kind of impression you might be making during the telephone screening. Is the energy level high or low? Are you asking for the face-to-face interview in the telephone phone screening? Do you sound disinterested in the position?

These are all reasons why a recruiter might screen out an applicant.

Are you addressing the potential weak points in your résumé in the cover letter or during the telephone interview?

If you are on a telephone screening and don't have a solid explanation for why, for example, you have had four jobs in two years, why you had an extended absence from the workforce, or why your GPA is low, the recruiter then might pull away.

In other words, know the potential weak spots in your career history and be ready to speak to those in the initial telephone screening.

The goal of many recruiters is to actually verify what they have seen on the résumé in the initial telephone screening.

The point to keep in mind is that a successful job search strategy will include many steps. Try to isolate and troubleshoot each step.

———

Skills and Competencies Checklists

Helping Skills	Rate yourself on a scale of 1 to 10 (*10 = highest level skills and 1 = lowest level skills*)	Actual example of WHEN and HOW you demonstrated this skill. (Consider a 4th column with the date you will begin to work on that skill or have examples).
Advocated		
Cared for		
Clarified		
Coached		
Collaborated		
Communicated		
Conducted		
Consoled		
Coordinated		
Counseled		
Demonstrated		
Developed		
Diagnosed		
Directed		
Empathized		
Empowered		
Encouraged		
Enlisted		
Evaluated		
Facilitated		
Guided		
Implemented		
Intervened		
Led		
Liaison		
Listened		
Mediated		
Merged		
Monitored		
Partnered		
Performed		
Personalized		
Problem solved		
Provided		
Questioned		
Referred		
Reflected		
Shared		
Started		
Supported		
Taught		
Trained		
Treated		
Uplifted		

Management Skills	Rate yourself on a scale of 1 to 10 (*10 = highest level skills and 1 = lowest level skills*)	Actual example of WHEN and HOW you demonstrated this skill. (Consider a 4th column with the date you will begin to work on that skill or have examples).
Administered		
Advised		
Analyzed		
Assessed		
Branded		
Budgeted		
Clarified		
Coached		
Collaborated		
Communicated		
Conducted		
Coordinated		
Counseled		
Decided		
Demonstrated		
Developed		
Diagnosed		
Directed		
Diversified		
Energized		
Engaged		
Evaluated		
Facilitated		
Fixed		
Implemented		
Included		
Intervened		
Led		
Liaison		
Listened		
Mediated		
Monitored		
Organized		
Oversaw		
Negotiated		
Partnered		
Performed		
Planned		
Promoted		
Provided		
Referred		
Spoke		
Started		
Supported		

Creative Skills	Rate yourself on a scale of 1 to 10 (*10 = highest level skills and 1 = lowest level skills*)	Actual example of WHEN and HOW you demonstrated this skill. (Consider a 4ᵗʰ column with the date you will begin to work on that skill or have examples).

Abstracted
Acted
Articulated
Authored
Brainstormed
Built
Conceptualized
Conceived
Conducted
Constructed
Created
Curated
Deduced
Demonstrated
Designed
Developed
Directed
Drafted
Fashioned
Ideate
Illustrated
Imagined
Inferred
Initiated
Innovated
Inspired
Integrated
Introduced
Made
Modified
Molded
Motivated
Performed
Planned
Produced
Published
Questioned
Shaped
Solved
Spoke
Started
Supported
Transformed
Translated

Coaching Skills	Rate yourself on a scale of 1 to 10 (*10 – highest level skills and 1 – lowest level skills*)	Actual example of WHEN and HOW you demonstrated this skill. (Consider a 4th column with the date you will begin to work on that skill or have examples).
Adapted		
Advocated		
Assisted		
Authored		
Briefed		
Challenged		
Changed		
Clarified		
Coached		
Communicated		
Contributed		
Coordinated		
Corrected		
Counseled		
Developed		
Directed		
Empowered		
Encouraged		
Energized		
Envisioned		
Evaluated		
Evolved		
Experimented		
Guided		
Improved		
Informed		
Initiated		
Instructed		
Interacted		
Invigorated		
Lectured		
Listened		
Mentored		
Motivated		
Prepared		
Supervised		
Supported		
Taught		
Trained		
Transformed		
Tutored		
Unified		
Ushered		
Visualized		

Detail Skills	Rate yourself on a scale of 1 to 10 (*10 = highest level skills and 1 = lowest level skills*)	Actual example of WHEN and HOW you demonstrated this skill. (Consider a 4th column with the date you will begin to work on that skill or have examples).
Accounted		
Analyzed		
Approved		
Arranged		
Audited		
Checked		
Classified		
Collected		
Compiled		
Consolidated		
Coordinated		
Corrected		
Detailed		
Discovered		
Dispatched		
Examined		
Executed		
Fine tuned		
Implemented		
Inspected		
Investigated		
Managed		
Measured		
Monitored		
Organized		
Planned		
Processed		
Quality control		
Questioned		
Reconciled		
Recorded		
Regulated		
Researched		
Resourced		
Responded		
Reported		
Retained		
Retrieved		
Reviewed		
Scheduled		
Summarized		
Synthesized		
Uncovered		
Wrote		

Manual Skills	Rate yourself on a scale of 1 to 10 (*10 = highest level skills and 1 = lowest level skills*)	Actual example of WHEN and HOW you demonstrated this skill. (Consider a 4th column with the date you will begin to work on that skill or have examples).
Assembled		
Bound		
Broke down		
Built		
Catalogued		
Cleaned		
Constructed		
Controlled		
Converted		
Coordinated		
Counted		
Covered		
Created		
Cut		
Delivered		
Designed		
Documented		
Drilled		
Drove		
Handled		
Inventoried		
Lifted		
Locked		
Mapped		
Maintained		
Manipulated		
Moved		
Operated		
Organized		
Patrolled		
Picked		
Pulled		
Received		
Registered		
Reorganized		
Repaired		
Relocated		
Restocked		
Routed		
Selected		
Set-up		
Shelved		
Shipped		
Sorted		

Research Skills	Rate yourself on a scale of 1 to 10 (*10 = highest level skills and 1 = lowest level skills*)	Actual example of WHEN and HOW you demonstrated this skill. (Consider a 4ᵗʰ column with the date you will begin to work on that skill or have examples).

Calculated
Clarified
Collaborated
Collected
Contributed
Controlled
Critiqued
Decided
Diagnosed
Documented
Evaluated
Examined
Expanded
Experimented
Extracted
Extrapolated
Filed
Gathered
Gleaned
Hypothesized
Identified
Informed
Inspected
Interpreted
Interviewed
Investigated
Isolated
Measured
Organized
Recognized
Reported
Resolved
Reviewed
Surveyed
Synthesized
Tabulated
Wrote
Clarified
Collected
Composed
Critiqued

Communication Skills	Rate yourself on a scale of 1 to 10 (*10 = highest level skills and 1 = lowest level skills*)	Actual example of WHEN and HOW you demonstrated this skill. (Consider a 4th column with the date you will begin to work on that skill or have examples).
Acknowledged		
Arbitrated		
Articulated		
Blogged		
Branded		
Clarified		
Collaborated		
Communicated		
Composed		
Created		
Delegated		
Developed		
Directed		
Discussed		
Explained		
Expressed		
Influenced		
Instructed		
Interfaced		
Interpreted		
Listened		
Marketed		
Mediated		
Motivated		
Negotiated		
Originated		
Paraphrased		
Partnered		
Persuaded		
Presented		
Processed		
Promoted		
Reasoned		
Reconciled		
Recruited		
Shared		
Sold		
Spoke		
Strategized		
Talked		
Transcribed		
Transitioned		
Tweeted (Social Media)		
Wrote		

Business Skills	Rate yourself on a scale of 1 to 10 (*10 = highest level skills and 1 = lowest level skills*)	Actual example of WHEN and HOW you demonstrated this skill. (Consider a 4ᵗʰ column with the date you will begin to work on that skill or have examples)
Allocated		
Analyzed		
Appraised		
Assigned		
Bought		
Branded		
Budgeted		
Calculated		
Closed		
Communicated		
Compromised		
Computed		
Connected		
Developed		
Documented		
Downsized		
Engaged		
Executed		
Expanded		
Initiated		
Insourced		
Lead		
Liquidated		
Maintained		
Managed		
Maximized		
Opened		
Operationalize		
Optimized		
Organized		
Outsourced		
Participated		
Planned		
Prepared		
Produced		
Promoted		
Realigned		
Recommended		
Researched		
Resolved		
Sold		
Solved		
Transferred		
Transformed		

SAMPLE RESUMES

Samonya V. Hourlie

1773 Bacon Drive, Stanfordville, NJ 08083 • Mobile 200.200.444. • Home: 444. • sam.hourlie@college.edu

CAREER OBJECTIVE

Participation in a competitive Management Training or Business Leadership program with the specific intention of developing a successful career in Sales, Marketing, Brand Management and/or Business Development.

EDUCATION & ACTIVITIES

CENTRAL UNIVERSITY of Indiana, Fort Wayne, GA
Bachelor of Science Degree in Business Administration, Concentration in Marketing, May 2014
Overall GPA 3.0, Dean's List, President's Scholar

- AACP Student Chapter (2011–2012)
- Library Archive Project Leader (Fall 2011)
- Graduation Usher (2004, 2010, 2011)
- Westingwell Fellowship (2011–Present)
- Business Club Member (2012–Present)
- Member AMA Student Chapter (2012)

SULLIMAN COMMUNITY COLLEGE, Loch, VA
Liberal Arts Major, Graduated May 2012
Overall GPA 3.56, Honors at Graduation

PROFESSIONAL EXPERIENCE

Resident Advisor—**Central University,** Fort Wayne, GA   Aug 2010–Present
- Assist and advise 300+students with daily collegiate life issues and oversee a wing of 20 male students
- Communicate news to residents, fellow RAs, and residence life directors on student accommodations
- Maintain a safe, clean, and socially balanced environment through meetings and conflict resolution sessions

Part-Time Telecommunications Sales Rep—**Phase Two Marketing,** Gibb, GA   Dec 2014–Present
- Enroll customers in various mobile phone plans; exceeded sales targets by 28 percent during the first month
- Selected to train and support new employees in sales strategies after two months with the company
- Offer existing customers new promotions and upgrade hundreds of walk-ins to keep location consistently in the region's top 3 producers

Standardized Test Evaluator Internship—**Miller Publishing,** Bogue, GA   Summers 2010-14
- Evaluated standardized test for grades 1 to 12 and verified that tests were graded accurately
- Checked for inconsistencies in questions and proofread marketing literature for distribution
- Fielded calls from vendors and clients and attempted to resolve issues based on company guidelines
- Conducted market research to identity potential reseller partnerships to develop new markets in the Midwest

SKILLS/VOLUNTEER WORK/INTERESTS

Computer: MS Office (Word, Excel, Power Point, Access), Windows 98, 2000, ME, XP, Internet, Email
Volunteer: 5K Run and Children without Borders (CWB) at Central University of Indiana (2011, 2012)
Interests: Entrepreneurship, Finance, Investing, History, Reading, Fishing, Chess, Weight Lifting, Football

Valerie Mathias

vmatthais@college.edu

		Cell 612.665.7516
College	524 College Circle | Campus District | GA | 16490	
Home	718 Aleppo Street | Aleppo Heights | IA | 16490	

OBJECTIVE: A part-time summer internship in broadcast journalism with specific interests in reporting and/or production.

EDUCATION: SIERRA SHAW UNIVERSITY, Campus District, FL
Bachelor of Arts in Communication, Junior Graduated: *May 2013*
Major: Communication Arts Minor: Journalism
Broadcasting Honors Program GPA: 3.2/4.0

ALEPPO COMMUNITY COLLEGE, Aleppo, FL
Associate of Arts in Liberal Studies Graduated: *May 2012*
Major: Liberal Studies
Dean's List, Second-Class Honors at Graduation

CAMPUS ACTIVITIES & LEADERSHIP:

- Society for Broadcasting Students, Vice President, 2010–2011
- WJSU Sierra University Radio Engineer, 2011–2012
- America's Young Journalism Society, member since Fall 2011
- Democracy Now campus volunteer, Spring and Fall 2011
- Campus Choirs, Volunteer, Spring 2011

PROFESSIONAL EXPERIENCE:

On-Air Host Jan 2012–Present WJSU, Campus Radio Station
- Anchor weekly 60-minute news show produced and run by Sierra University students
- Report live from many campus events including the annual Fall Rush Day or Salute to Seniors
- Narrated new DVD and CD-ROM marketing promotions for department's student recruiting video

Broadcast Intern Summer 2011 Power 104, WJOK, New York
- Booked guests, 18–24 years to debate and discuss controversial current affairs issues
- Assembled and edited video clips of entertainment events for 60-second preview spots
- Assisted staff of 5 with operations and production-related issues on remotes

Junior Camp Counselor Summers 2014, 2010 Young Girls of Iowa, Troop 74, IA
- Assisted troop leaders to coordinate summer camp activities for children aged 7 to 12 years
- Mentored up to seven young girls in an assigned cluster through age appropriate programs
- Performed Lead Chaperone duties on trips ensuring safety and well-being of all campers

SPECIAL SKILLS & LANGUAGES:
Excellent writing skills; 50 WPM
Basic knowledge of Haitian Creole and Spanish
Administrative, Marketing and Public Relations experience working in family business for 6 years

John R. Franklin

252 West Great House Circle / Whittier / CA / 91210 / Phone 405.405.1111

OBJECTIVE: Accounting Associate or Clerk in a small to midsize business.

PERSONAL QUALIFICATIONS:

Math skills/Accounting Software	*Team Player*	*Customer Service Oriented*
Professional Interaction	*Determined to Succeed*	*Dedicated and Responsible*
Focused Problem Solver	*Detail Oriented*	*Self-Motivated*

EDUCATION & INTERNSHIP:

Point A&M University, High Point, NC
Degree—Business Administration   Anticipated graduation, May 2013
18-month internship program; 75 percent self-funded college; Dean's List
   o   Bank Statement Reconciliation, Tax Filing
   o   General Ledger, Payroll on ADP
   o   Peachtree, QuickBooks, MS Excel/Access, Intuit, Turbo Tax

WORK EXPERIENCE:

Customer Service/Data Specialist, 04/13–12/13   Alliance One, High Point, NC
   o   Advised customers of errors or changes to accounts and the required remedy to resolve issues
   o   Met quotas while exceeding required minimum 250 accounts daily with a 100 % accuracy
   o   Completed necessary changes on accounts when mistakes were detected
   o   Entered new data and sent e-mails and faxes out to coworkers and customers when needed
   o   Recognized for using good judgment to restore or disconnect cable, telephone and Internet accounts

Mail Room Clerk, 03/12–04/12   Internal Revenue, High Point, NC
   o   Unbundled confidential envelopes containing official government documents and transcripts
   o   Opened and separated 550+ documents daily containing checks of $500–$1,000

Seasonal Sales Associate, 05/12–08/12   Big Jobs, High Point, NC
   o   Assisted 150+ customers daily with merchandise selections, and pricing
   o   Merchandised and stocked shelves; helped customers take purchases to cars
   o   Maintained overall cleanliness of store, also operated cash register

Seasonal Package Handler, 11/11–12/11   United Parcel, Los Angeles, CA
   o   Delivered packages to homes and obtained customer signatures
   o   Used scanners to input and reroute undeliverable packages

Produce Clerk, 04/11–05/11   Shop Rite, Los Angeles, CA
   o   Maintained food inventory levels and stocked shelves with fresh produce
   o   Assisted customers with questions and product selections

Sabina Park

26 Old South Camp Road, Belvoir Heights, CT 19004 • 657.657. • sabinapark@mail.com

Help Desk Technician

Skilled Help Desk Technician with 5 years of experience providing PC and Client/Server tech support for small to medium-size businesses. Experience diagnosing, troubleshooting and resolving client issues with hardware maintenance, installations, and upgrades. Experienced in technical call center operations providing service by communicating effectively with technical and nontechnical staff during citywide winter emergencies

Qualifications & Education

A+ Certified Technician, 2014
MCP Certification, 2014
Bachelor of Science in Business Administration, Riverside City College, 2013
AST in Electronic Engineering Technology, Sumpter College, 2011

Hardware

IBM compatible PCs, Sun Workstations, Ethernet, Cisco Routers, Video & Sound Cards, CD-ROM Drives, Multiplexors, HP and Xerox printing systems

Operating Systems / Applications

Windows XP/2000/NT/98/95, Microsoft Exchange, Novell, DOS, TCP/IP, UNIX; ERP, SAP, HRIS, JAVA, HTML

Professional Experience

Help Desk Technician, Riverside Consulting, Hartford, CT   Oct 2010 to Present
Riverside Consulting provides technology services to city municipalities and schools

- Provide desktop support for over 120 clients in the greater Hartford region by phone or in person as needed to minimize downtime
- Plan and lead training sessions for new and existing clients as part of the "Lion Team" initiative; facilitate at least 3 sessions per month
- Support as necessary on a 24-7 basis to limit system down time during internal or external outages and peak enrollment periods
- Identify, isolate and repair computer equipment showing wear and tear as well as during preventative maintenance routines

Membership & Affiliations

Hartford Tech Circle, member since June 2010
Association of Help Desk Professionals, member since December 2011
Hartford T-Ball Circle of Champions League, part-time coach and mentor since 2012

Samonya Hourlie

5100 North 3rd Street, Anytown, GA 19106 / Phone 610 555 0096 / sam.hourlie@mail.com

OBJECTIVE

Supervisory position in the Hospitality field offering opportunities for advancement and professional development in a company recognized for customer relations and event management excellence.

SKILLS PROFILE

- Certified Conflict Resolution and Mediation Officer since Aug 2011
- Recognized by managers for detail orientation and multitasking abilities
- Proven ability to balance competing priorities and tight deadlines
- Developed a reputation for quality of work and timely completion of projects
- Completed Customer Service Level II and III Hospitality training
- Certificate of Completion in the 4-week Supervisory Skills Workshop series

EMPLOYMENT HISTORY

The Family Hotel & Suites, Anytown, GA   May 2012–Present
Front Desk & Guest Services Operator

- Maintain upscale environment for all hotel guests and conference patrons
- Train and monitor new hires in daily front desk processes and operations
- Coordinate conference and meeting space allocation based on needs and handle event planning issues

Soft Drink Bottling Group, Anytown, GA   Feb 2010–Apr 2012
Customer Service Floater

- Performed administrative and customer service work in multiple departments including operations, sales and customer call center
- Assisted Human Resources department to coordinate new employee orientations, community mentoring programs and monthly staff recognition events
- Recognized as Employee-of-the-Month, twice in three years for outstanding work based on customer and vendor feedback

Teen & Tots Recreation Center, Anytown, GA   May 2009–Jan 2010
Camp Associate

- Enforced rules and regulations of recreational facilities to maintain discipline and ensure safety for guests ranging in age from 5 to 17 years
- Managed the daily operations of recreational facilities with 4 other team members
- Administered first aid/CPR, and notified emergency personnel when necessary

EDUCATION

Andrew Jackson High School, Mead, PA
High school diploma, May 2009
Courses—Business Basics, Office Administration, MS Office

COMMUNITY

Cultured Youth, Cofounder and President since 2011
Organize and plan trips for up to 20 teens to museums, plays and community theatre.

CORDIA WHITESTONE

Phone 613.613. | 4684 Taburst Trail, Decatur, GA 30034 | cordiawhitestone@gmail.com

OBJECTIVE

College sophomore with interest in arts and entertainment seeks a summer internship opportunity in North Carolina, South Carolina, or Georgia.

EDUCATION

Blandin University, Orangeburg, SC
Bachelor of Science in Business Administration, May 2016—**GPA 3.1**
Courses: Financial Accounting, Business Communications, Microeconomics, and Spanish

HONORS/AWARDS/SCHOLARSHIPS

2013–2014 Scholarship Recipient
United Negro College Fund (UNCF); Blandin University Focus; Blandin University Hats & Gloves

CAMPUS INVOLVEMENT

- **Pre Alumni Council**   Supporting institutional advancement programs
- **NAACP**   Caldwell University campus chapter
- **Sigma Alpha Pi**   National Society of Leadership and Success

PROFESSIONAL EXPERIENCE

Peer Counselor, **BLANDIN UNIVERSITY**, *Orangeburg, SC*   Aug 2013–Present
- Schedule tutorial sessions with 4–15 students weekly
- Record weekly progress of the students in the program
- Promote freshman success by directly supporting 9 students

Sales Associate, **COLLEGE BOOKSTORE**, *Clarkston, GA*   Dec 2012–Jan 2013
- Handled monetary transactions; recorded sales at the end of my shift
- Marketed and merchandized sale items throughout the store

Cashier, **ROMANO'S PIZZA**, *Stone Mountain, GA*   Aug 2011–Mar 2012
- Processed payments; maintained cleanliness of the front end of the restaurant
- Greeted each customer and provided great customer service

COMMUNITY SERVICE

Project Life: Riverview Elementary tutor; National Bone Marrow Association donor; American Red Cross donor; Springfield Memorial AME Church Thanksgiving Program Volunteer

COMPUTER SKILLS

Microsoft Word, PowerPoint, Excel, Publisher, Access; Internet Research; Social Media

Ronesha R. Landing

111 Singapore Lane, Stephen, SC 29479 / 888-444-2149 / rrrlanding4@gmail.com

PROFESSIONAL OBJECTIVE

Seeking a full-time opportunity where seven years of customer service experience, office administrative skills, education in business and technology along with excellent communication skills and a strong work ethic, will support professional growth and career advancement within a progressive organization.

EDUCATION & RECENT TRAINING

Bachelor of Science, Computer Science, Bennett College for Women, NC   2009 to 2012
Associate of Arts, Business Administration, American Intercontinental University, IL   2005 to 2009
High school diploma, Timberland County High School, SC   2002 to 2006

SPECIAL SKILLS

Computer Science courses	AA Degree in Business	7 years customer service
Help desk experience	Microsoft Office Proficient	Visual Studio, C++
Staff training/supervision	Retail Operations	Project management
Troubleshooting	Strong work ethic	Quick learner
Keyboarding 40 WPM	Computer Networks	Social Media

WORK EXPERIENCE

Administrative Assistant, Department of Social Services, SC   Jan 2013 to Jul 2013
Berkeley County Department of Social Services Economics Division
- Handle highly regulated, document flow processes—filing, copying, shredding, and scanning
- Take high volume of inbound calls and route for social workers depending on client needs
- Work with clients via telephone as directed and within department policies and guidelines
- Track cases and complete report spreadsheets on staff activities using Microsoft Excel

Customer Sales Associate, Multiple Retail Part Time, SC   Oct 2006 to Jan 2012
Lowes Home Improvement, Bath & Body Works and Victoria Secret Store locations
- Lowes Stores: 3 years in customer services, scheduled service deliveries and return desk
- Bath & Body Works: 5 years in a busy mall location; trained new hires and opened/closed
- Victoria Secret: 1-year part-time mall location; worked with customers in high-end lingerie sales

Customer Service Claims Representative, ESecuritel TelePerformance   Jul 2006 to Oct 2006
- Received and handled inbound calling for claims for lost, stolen and damaged telephones
- Routed telephone calls based on client complaint and needs to ensure highest level of customer support
- Completed training on company customer service guidelines and response processes

Computer Lab Assistant, Bennett College for Women, NC   Sep 2003 to May 2005
Funded through HBCU grants from National Science Foundation
- Employed and trained by IT Services to work in campus computer lab handling technical support issues
- Assisted students, staff with computer assignments and worked with IT to ensure equipment operational
- Authorized to remote access into student computers to troubleshoot network, login or application issues

VOLUNTEER/COMMUNITY

Rescue Savior Baptist Church Youth Ministry Advisor   Nov 2007 to Current
*Assist with devotion, homework, classroom and youth program activities

Reza Robinson

Campus: Building #193, Carey Drive, Apartment #7B, Lincoln PA 19382
Home: 1711 Brians Way, Norriscity, PA 19003 | 949.949. | rr198021@spu.edu

EDUCATION/TRAINING
Spring Prairie University of Pennsylvania

Major—Philosophy (3.5) Minor in Political Science (3.4)
Junior Status. Anticipating graduation in May 2014
Completed 12-week radio training program and spring semester as a DJ at WXUR
Completed Communications Practicum

Burland County Community College, Baltimore, MD

Major—Liberal Studies, September 2010 to May 2011, Freshman Year, GPA 3.3
Peer Mentor Training on goal setting, time management, and campus resources Spring 2011

ACTIVITIES | CLASSES | VOLUNTEER
- Blogger, Creative Writer
- College Peer Mentor
- WCUR (University Radio)
- Member of WXUR music committee
- Member, Philosophy Club (2011–2012)
- Music Reviewer
- Contributor, Art and Music Magazine
- Volunteer at Safe Space Shelter
- Volunteer at Books through Bars
- Writer, *The Quad* campus newspaper

SPECIAL SKILLS | ABILITIES
Computer Savvy   Project Research   Strong Work Ethic
Good Communication skills   Social Media Marketing   Uses Initiative

WORK EXPERIENCE
Sales Associate   Spiegels Music Store   **10/2012 to Present**
- Order, ship, receive, and sell inventory. Resolve vendor and customer issues.

Sales Associate   SSI Bookstore, Spring Prairie University, PA   **1/2012 to 5/2012**
- Organized shelves, shipped/received inventory, resolved vendor and customer issues in person, via phone, or e-mail.

Peer Mentor   Spring County Community College, PA   **1/2011 to 8/2011**
- Part of 15-person community college peer-mentor team that resolved student issues.
- Conducted several workshops; worked on department initiatives.
- Worked with college advisors, faculty, and student affairs professionals to resolve student enrollment, technical advising, and registration issues.

Najiyyah C. McCloud

3450 N. Harrison Street, Wilmington, DE 19802 302 402 4242 najiyyah@gmail.com

PROFESSIONAL PROFILE / CAREER OBJECTIVE

Dynamic, energetic professional with excellent people skills and sound knowledge of Allied Health roles, wants to bring education, experience, and training to a new challenge in the Human Services profession. With 7+ years of direct customer service experience and 6+ years in Nanotechnology, this professional has demonstrated the ability to work successfully in detail-oriented, time-sensitive environments within the health-care sector to meet organizational needs. Pursuing career change to focus on advocacy for individual or community health and behavioral wellness.

EDUCATION/TRAINING/SKILLS

Bachelor of Science in Behavioral Science, Delaware State University, Graduating August 2011
Relevant coursework—Psychology, Interpersonal Relations, Sociology, Human Behavior

Associate Degree in Allied Health, Delaware Technical & Community College, Completed May 2005
Certificate in Health Career Studies, Delaware Technical & Community College

PROFESSIONAL SKILLS

- 8+ years of customer service
- Excellent interpersonal skills
- Organized, creative, and driven
- Motivate and support individuals
- Microsoft Office Suite/MAC products
- Ability to follow written/verbal instructions
- Work effectively independently or with team

TECHNICAL SKILLS

- Microscopic evaluation of tissue for Nanotech
- Knowledge of biology, chemistry, physiology
- Applying meticulous attention to detail
- Ability to follow laboratory protocols
- Knowledge of precision lab equipment
- Ability to interpret regulatory information
- Medical and lab terminology

PROFESSIONAL EXPERIENCE

UNIVERSITY OF RALEIGH—Dermatology   **Histotechnologist II**   02/08–05/11
- Worked as one of six Nanotech lab technicians working with supervisory staff to complete assignments in the main Dermatology lab at one of the nation's premier research and training university.
- Followed established department and industry protocols to prepare, cut, and stain tissue specimens for microscopic examination by pathologists in a timely manner; worked rotational shifts.
- Used guidelines to troubleshoot tissue identification and tissue slide preparations.

WESTERN COUNTY HOSPITAL—Surgical Lab   **Histotechnologist II**   10/05–02/08
- Earned ASCP Certification from the National Society of Nanotechnologic Technicians
- Performed quality control (QC) on finished slide preparation and maintained required documentation of all procedures and laboratory equipment.
- Prepared slides of body tissue for microscopic examination by freezing and cutting tissues, mounting them on slides and staining them with special dyes to make them visible under a microscope for medical diagnosis.

WTRS BANK/ ONE FEDERAL CU—Wilmington   **Financial Associate**   01/98–01/05
- Worked with customers to open or upgraded accounts and sold products or services based on client needs.
- Developed and updated detailed financial records; used financial reporting data to resolve issues.

PROFESSIONAL AFFILIATIONS / COMMUNITY

American Society for Clinical Pathology, Member since 2005
ASCP Certification from the National Society of Histology Technician, October 2005
Volunteer associate for Adult Literacy Program

THANNEL F. CHINNAWAY
www.LinkedIn.com/in/thannelchinnaway
| 259.259.7615 | thannelchinnaway@gmail.com |

CAREER OBJECTIVE
To engage in productive work that fuels my personal passion to innovate and problem solve in creative ways, motivate and support team members, and engage community while growing professionally. Industries of interest: Consumer Affairs, Health & Wellness, Hospitality & Tourism, Real Estate and Technology.

SUMMARY OF QUALIFICATIONS
Communications, marketing, and management self-starter with 5+ years of administrative, entrepreneurial, customer relations, and event coordination experience with nonprofits and private businesses; excellent team player, strong relationship builder, project manager and creative leader who has experience successfully organizing and planning communications, marketing, research, product development/launch projects for small business success.

EDUCATION & SKILLS
Parks University of Pennsylvania, Graduated May 2015
Bachelor of Science Degree in Marketing, *Dean's List Recognition 2012, 2013, and 2014*

- *Urban Marketing*
- *Retailing & Sales*
- *International Business*
- *Consumer Behavior*
- *Community Activist*

- *Business Development*
- *Entrepreneurship*
- *Event Management*
- *Personnel Management*
- *Public Speaker*

- *Social Media Proficient*
- *Technology Savvy*
- *Excellent Writer*
- *Team Builder & Coach*
- *Organizer*

PROFESSIONAL EXPERIENCES

1954 Commons, Marketing Consultant   Jan 2014–Present
Provider of marketing, public relations and business development services to nonprofits
- Work with 2 small business clients on public relations strategy and brand marketing, social media and writing services to achieve stated organizational goals.
- Assist clients with proactive media relations efforts, comprehensive range of marketing initiatives including direct marketing, product research, product distribution, assemble and liaise with creative design teams.

The Blues Box Foundation, Literacy Coordinator Intern   May 2013–Present
Nonprofit community organization to nurture college-bound students of color, artistically and academically
- Participated as the Literacy Program Coordinator for the Summer 2013 initiative to promote academic excellence and intellectual growth.
- Program Volunteer: Phenomenally University, Camp Esteban, Journey into Dyslexia, Made in America Festival, 2013 Tails Picnic and Literacy Love Learning.

Deck & Chili's, Server   Apr 2012–Present
$1.1Billion venues that combine entertainment and dining in North America for both adults and families
- Consistently employed throughout college experience to deliver an unparalleled guest experience through the best combination of food, drinks, and games.
- Collaborate with a high-energy team to create a warm, fun atmosphere for guests and staff in a fast-paced restaurant environment.
- Resolves customer issues as they arise and works with managers to resolve guest services issues in the least disruptive manner possible.

LAMAR JOEL ROWAN

1700 W. Susquehanna Ave, Philadelphia, PA 19121 | LJR@gmail.com | 267.267.1234 | LinkedIn.com/LJR

PROFESSIONAL OBJECTIVE

Ambitious, determined and capable graduating senior with Mock Trial and Jurist Academy experience seeks enrollment in distinguished, competitive law program in a challenging environment supporting professional growth and excellence.

SPECIAL SKILLS / COMPETENCIES

Resourceful	*Widely Read*	*Campus Leader*	*Organized*
Strong Work Ethic	*Relationship Builder*	*Dependable/Reliable*	*Motivated*
Community Involved	*Good Communicator*	*Excellent Team Player*	*Determined*

EDUCATION / ACADEMIC ACCOMPLISHMENTS

CARROLLTON UNIVERSITY of Pennsylvania, Carroll, PA
Bachelor of Arts Degree in Social Relations—Concentration in Criminal Justice
Anticipated Graduation May 2013; *GPA 3.06*
Coursework—American Political Systems, Sports Law, Hospitality Law, Quantitative Methods in Social Research, Noninstitutional Treatment of Offenders
Jurist Academy, Wiltham College Summer 2012
Graduated in the top 25 percent of high school & Mock Trial Club

CAMPUS LEADERSHIP EXPERIENCE

Vice President, Student Government Cooperative Association (SGCA)—Junior Year 2011 to 2012
Vice President, Student Organization Against Poverty (SOAP), Senior Year 2012 to 2013
Who's Who Among American Colleges and Universities, Spring 2012

INTERNSHIPS / COLLEGE RESEARCH PROJECTS

Campus Police Intern   **Summer 2012**, Carrollton University Police, Carroll PA
- Provided support to team of Patrol Officers, Residence Life staff and Police Dispatchers.
- Worked on team project to implement and enhance safety training guidelines for student residents.

Academic Projects   **2011 and 2012, Social Relations Research & Data Projects**
- The Divergent Comfort Level Felt by Men vs. Women Working with Ex-Convicts
- Performance of Minorities on the LSAT

WORK EXPERIENCE

May 2009 to Present	**Head Cashier,** Comevack Corporation, Philadelphia, PA
Sep 2007 to May 2009	**Cashier,** Spendway Pharmacy, Philadelphia, PA

- Work consistently through high school and college; Supervise 4 cashiers and front-end activities
- Ensure customer service standards are met; monitor entrance, exit doors; assist with loss prevention

TECHNICAL/SKILLS/COMMUNITY

Computer: Microsoft Office (Word, Excel, Power Point, Access), Windows 98, 2000, ME, XP, Internet
Interests: Public Administration, Criminal Justice, Community Affairs
Community: Chosen 300 Ministries & Boys and Girls Club of Chester, PA

Quick Start Résumé Worksheet!

Name_____

Address_____ | Phone_____ | E-mail_____

OBJECTIVE
_____
_____

EDUCATION /TRAINING

Name of College, City, State _____
Type of degree _____ Graduation month, year_____ GPA _____

Other Educational Institution
Name of School, City, State _____
Outcome_____ Completion month, year_____ GPA _____

SPECIAL SKILLS

List all hardware/software/technology skills and computer application knowledge
Languages—bilingual English/_____
Keyboarding 30 wpm (www.typingtest.com)_____

Keyword...	Skills...	Buzz words...

WORK (Professional) EXPERIENCE (include relevant paid or unpaid)

Company Name_____, City, State _____ Dates_____
Job Title_____
Use complete sentences to describe what you have done at this job:
_____
_____
_____

Company Name_____, City, State _____ Dates_____
Job Title_____
Use complete sentences to describe what you have done at this job:
_____
_____
_____